*Collective Bargaining and
the Public Interest*

Collective Bargaining and the Public Interest

A Welfare Economics Assessment

DAVID M. WINCH

McGill-Queen's University Press
Kingston, Montreal, London

©McGill-Queen's University Press 1989
ISBN 0-7735-0696-9

Legal deposit first quarter 1989
Bibliothèque nationale du Québec

∞

Printed in Canada on acid-free paper

This book has been published with the help of a grant
from the Social Science Federation of Canada, using
funds provided by the Social Sciences and Humanities
Research Council of Canada.

Canadian Cataloguing in Publication Data

Winch, David M., 1933–
    Collective bargaining and the public interest
    Includes index.
    Bibliography: p.
    ISBN 0-7735-0696-9
    1. Collective bargaining—Canada.
    2. Trade-unions—Canada. I. Title.
    HD6524.W56 1989   331.89'0971   C89-090033-7

Contents

Preface

Very few of our economic policies are as important as those that govern the operation of the labour market. Efficient use of our labour resources is vital to our economic prosperity, while relative wage rates govern the way the products of our society are shared among its members. Conflict in the labour market is daily news and major work stoppages are of concern to workers, consumers, and governments. Unemployment is a perennial problem. The procedures of collective bargaining that characterize the labour market today, including the conflict phase of strike and lock-out, are governed by legislation. The whole process must accordingly be viewed as one that has been chosen by policy, and the outcome of the process must be seen as the consequence of that policy. When current policy provides for the creation of major problems, it is necessary to ask whether our chosen policy is the best possible. This book addresses precisely that issue.

The forces at work in the labour market, the possible structures of the market, and the criteria by which performance should be judged are all complex issues. Only after they have been analysed is it possible to formulate well-founded recommendations for policy. If brevity and rigour were the only considerations, my analysis would have been developed and presented in the technical language of economic theory. But it would then have been readable only by professional economists. I have chosen instead to use plain language wherever possible, for the issues are of concern to all and the argument should be accessible to all. Some compromise has been necessary and I crave the indulgence of the reader. Economists may find what to them are well-known concepts developed at apparently ex-

cessive length. Others are asked to accept the use of some un-
familiar technical terms and to follow the discussion of their
meaning. The reward for all readers is the promise of conclusions that address the problems caused by our current procedures and policies in the labour market and recommendations
that offer significant improvement.

The conclusions follow from the analysis. While some of the
conclusions and recommendations will not be popular with
some readers, they can be rejected fairly only if it can be argued either that my premises are unacceptable or that my reasoning is unsound. I do not, of course, claim to have written
the perfect book, to have discovered perfect policy, or to have
reached incontrovertible conclusions. But I do claim to have
derived my conclusions from thorough analysis and to have justified my recommendations by reasoned argument. I hope that
my critics will similarly offer reasoned criticism, rather than
simple rejection, and that they will attempt to base contrary
recommendations on careful analysis of the issues. If this book
initiates serious debate, and the eventual result is some improvement in the way we manage our labour resources, then it
will have served its purpose, whether or not all my recommendations are adopted.

*Collective Bargaining and
the Public Interest*

CHAPTER ONE

Introduction

> The mechanism by which the wages and other
> employment conditions of the labour force are
> determined is clearly one of the most
> fundamental choices for a society to make. The
> mechanism will affect the total income and
> wealth generated by the economy and the
> distribution of that income and wealth among
> members of society.
>
> W.C. Riddell, *Canadian Labour Relations.*

In Canada today, the labour market is widely perceived as dominated by trade unions, the process of collective bargaining, and the resolution of disputes by strikes. The attention of the public is focused, largely by the news media, on the determination of wages by the collective bargaining process. In fact, approximately one-half of the paid employees eligible for unionization have their wages determined by collective bargaining between employers and unions.[1] The proportion of nonagricultural paid workers who are members of certified unions increased from about 25 per cent in 1945 to about 40 percent in 1983. Since only some 86 per cent of employees whose wages are determined by collective agreements are union members, close to one-half of the eligible labour force is governed by the process. While union membership in Canada has increased since the Second World War, it has declined in the USA since the 1960s to less than 20 per cent of nonagricultural workers in 1983, well below the 35 per cent membership in 1945.[2] Much of the growth in Canada is attributable to extensive unionization of the public sector, though unionization in the private sector has also grown in Canada, while it has declined in the USA.[3]

The influence of the collective bargaining process is more extensive than its coverage. Many associations of employees that are not certified unions negotiate wages with their employers, and the trend of wage settlements in collective agreements serves as an example for wage settlements where no certified union exists. It is true that in Canada today the labour market is dominated by the process of collective bargaining. Its impact is far from uniform, however. Unions do succeed in raising the real wages of their members and this is at the expense, directly or indirectly, of those members of society who are not unionized.[4] It is little wonder that unions, collective bargaining, and strikes are matters of widespread concern among the public.

Public opinion has been assessed by a number of polls, which show a change in attitude towards unions in recent years. "The Gallup Poll has, since 1950, asked respondents whether they think labour unions are good or bad for Canada. In the 1950–58 period, between 12 and 20 per cent answered 'bad' and between 60 and 69 per cent 'good' ... However, in the 1976–82 period, between 30 and 42 per cent answered 'bad' and between 42 and 52 per cent 'good.'[5] The increased negative opinion of unions may be due to the more frequent use of strikes to resolve disputes. "Canadians, according to public opinion polls, are becoming increasingly intolerant of strikes, especially in certain public services ... Public opinion polls suggest that a majority of Canadians, including those in households with a union member, think that strikes called by labour unions are not even beneficial to union members."[6]

More Canadians are now concerned about the power of unions than are worried by big business or big government. "Nearly two-thirds of Canadians (65 per cent) think that unions are becoming too powerful ... In 1980 a public opinion poll revealed that 36 per cent of Canadians consider 'big labour' a threat to the future well-being of Canada. 'Big business' was believed to be a threat by 20 per cent of Canadians while 29 per cent expressed the opinion that 'big government is the biggest threat to Canada's future.'"[7] "Another recent Decima question asked respondents whether they favoured or opposed greater government control over labour union activity. More than 60 per cent favoured more control; even among union members a majority favoured increased government control over labour union activity."[8]

The opinion of unions held by Canadians is not wholly negative, however. While they are concerned about the use of strikes and the impact that excessive wage demands may have on the rate of inflation and level of unemployment, they view with favour the role of unions in protecting workers form exploitation and in improving working conditions. In a recent survey of residents in Edmonton and Winnipeg, Krahn and Lowe[9] found that "a majority of respondents agreed that unionized employees enjoy better wages and working condi-

tions than non-union employees. A slightly larger proportion
of respondents agreed with the statements, 'We need more laws
to limit the power of unions,' 'Labour unions should be regulated to a greater extent by the government,' 'Unions impose
too many restrictions on employers' and [there was] substantial agreement with the statement 'the high wage demands of
unions contribute directly to inflation.'"[10] This ambivalence is
reflected in other studies. "Public perception of unions generally cluster into two groups: a negative big-labour image owing
to a pervasive belief that 'unions help cause inflation,' and a
positive instrumental view that unions are 'an effective mechanism for gaining improvements in wages and working conditions.'"[11] "In response to a recent Decima question forcing
respondents to choose between the statements 'unions in Canada have become too powerful' and 'unions are necessary in
Canada to protect workers from exploitation,' over 55 per cent
of respondents chose 'too powerful', and 45 per cent 'necessary.'"[12] Similar attitudes have been revealed by studies in the
USA "a substantial majority of respondents saw US unions as
being large, politically powerful, and unrepresentative institutions, that is, they had a largely negative view of unions and
society. At the same time, the vast majority of respondents
agreed that unions improve the wages and job security of their
members and protect workers against unfair practices."[13]
The public attitude that views some of the activities of
unions favourably, while being concerned about the consequences of collective bargaining and strikes, coincides with the conclusions of academic studies of the economic effects of the
procedures currently used in the labour market. Economists
tend to focus on the economic costs associated with conflict,
production lost during work stoppages, and the inefficiency
caused by the use of the monopoly power of unions to raise
wage rates in some occupations more than in others. They
view the process of collective bargaining and the outcome as
costly and inefficient. Most authorities agree that these aspects
of the collective bargaining process do indeed impose inefficiency costs on society.[14] Many of the activities of unions have
favourable consequences, however. The organized voice of workers places them on a more equal footing with management
in discussions of employment conditions and efficient deploy-
ment of the labour force in the production process.[15]
The continuous debate about the harm or good that unions
do to our society has largely been at cross purposes. Critics

of unions focus on the inefficiency costs, while advocates of unions emphasize their positive contributions. Authorities who recognize that both sides have valid arguments differ about the nature of the important question. Freeman and Medoff, in their concluding chapter, say, "in our view, there is some truth to both sides of the debate. The central question is not, 'who in principle is right?' but rather, 'which face is quantitatively more important in particular economic outcomes?'"[16] Their conclusion is that on balance unions probably do more good than harm. Their "central question" would, of course, be the relevant one if the issue were whether to retain the activities of unions in their present form or to abolish unions altogether. Riddell raises the more interesting problem: "The evidence indicates that unions have both costs and benefits for society. The challenge for public policy is to increase the benefits and reduce the costs."[17] How the benefits yielded by the activities of unions can be enhanced lies outside the scope of this study, but the chapters that follow will be centrally concerned with the harm done to the economy by unions, collective bargaining, and labour market conflict, and how that harm can be reduced.

Estimating the magnitude of the harm done is extremely difficult because both the process and the outcome of collective bargaining have ramifications throughout the economy. Four aspects of the problem can be identified, but none of them is simple to isolate and measure. First is the value of output lost because of work stoppages by strikes and lock-outs. Second is the inefficiency cost or deadweight loss caused by distortions in the allocation of labour and capital that result from higher wages in sectors dominated by powerful unions and lower wages elsewhere. Third is the cost of unemployment caused by the maintenance of high real wage rates. Finally there is the cost to society of the inequity that results from increased wages in some occupations, depressed wages in others, and the exclusion from the labour market of some potential workers, especially young workers. Data on the value of lost output can never reflect the human costs borne by the disgruntled and the frustrated.

Data are available on the amount of working time lost by strikes and lock-outs. Over the period 1966 to 1983, .34 per cent of working time was lost in Canada.[18] The loss of output due to strikes and lock-outs is more difficult to estimate. If time lost is offset by overtime working either before or after the stoppage, or if output would have been reduced by layoffs if it had not been reduced by strikes, then the proportion of output lost would be less than the proportion of working time lost. Further output is lost, however, by the effect of work stoppages on suppliers and customers of the firm closed down. The data on strikes include only those on strike or locked-out, not those in related firms whose output is reduced. Thus the proportion of working time lost may either overestimate or underestimate the proportion of output lost. If the errors are offsetting, then the cost of strikes and lock-outs to the economy is in the order of .3 to .4 per cent of output.

The magnitude of the deadweight loss is estimated differently in different research studies. On the basis of a US study by De Fina,[19] Riddell estimates the deadweight loss in Canada to be in the order of .2 per cent of GNP,[20] arguing that it is higher in Canada than in the USA. However, Freeman and Medoff estimate the loss in the USA to be .2 to .4 per cent of GNP.[21]

The extent to which unemployment is caused by high real wage rates achieved by the power of unions is controversial and difficult to assess. Certainly unions are not entirely to blame when there is a 10 per cent unemployment rate. The unemployment rate responds to the pace of economic activity and to changes in the rate of inflation, which leads economists to isolate the natural or nonaccelerating inflation rate of unemployment (NAIRU). The NAIRU has increased in Canada from 4 to 5 per cent in the 1950s to 6 to 8 per cent in the early 1980s.[22] Various studies have attempted to identify the extent to which the change can be attributed to demographic trends, technological and economic change, revisions to the Unemployment Insurance Act, and increases in real minimum wages.[23] What these studies really demonstrate is that the labour market and the structure of wage rates in the economy has been insufficiently flexible to accommodate the impact of changes in demography, technology, and policy. If union power increases or maintains real wage rates when other forces would tend to reduce them, then such pressures will result in unemployment. Whether the unemployment is then caused by the union power or other pressures is a pointless debate. If either were not present, the unemployment rate would be lower.

The optimum rate for the NAIRU is not zero. In an efficient labour market there must be some mobility. Search takes time and there will always be some people transitionally unemployed between jobs, just as in an efficient housing market there is a vacancy rate of apartments empty between tenants. But the unemployment rate that would accommodate efficient mobility and search need not exceed 2 to 3 per cent. When the NAIRU is 6 to 8 per cent we still have 4 to 5 per cent of the labour force unemployed because the labour market is imperfect and unable to adjust rapidly to changing circumstances. In recent years there has been a resurgence of interest among economists in the basic truths of classical economics. One of those basics truths is that the only reason a person fails to find a job after a reasonable period of search is because no employer would find it profitable to employ him at current wage rates. More employment would be profitable at lower real wage rates. The NAIRU would be lower if wage rates were not maintained at such high real levels by the power of unions through the collective bargaining process. It is not unreasonable to estimate that the excess of the NAIRU over an efficient rate of unemployment for purposes of mobility and search might be halved if we could overcome the problem of high real wage rates. In that case, the consequence of the current process of wage determination is an excess unemployment rate of some 2 to 2.5 per cent.

The level of GNP is not proportionally related to the unemployment rate. There are three reasons for supposing that a reduction in the unemployment rate by 1 per cent would raise GNP by less than 1 per cent. First, one consequence of high real wage rates is that new entrants to the labour force find it particularly difficult to find employment. In Canada the youth unemployment rate over the last twenty years has been over twice the adult rate.[24] Second, the unemployment rate among adults is greatest for workers with low levels of education and skill. Thus a reduction in unemployment would add to the working population young and unskilled workers who are less productive than those currently employed. Finally, an increase in the number of persons employed, with no change in the capital stock, would not increase output proportionally because the marginal product of labour is lower than the average product.[25]

There are, however, counter arguments to each of these three reasons. Youths are less productive than adults because they are inexperienced. The sooner they find work, the sooner they gain experience. Over a working life the person who starts work one month earlier contributes an additional month of work as an experienced adult. The long-run effect of reducing the youth unemployment rate is to increase the working life span. The gain in output immediately is the productivity of youth, but in the long-run it is the productivity of an experienced worker. Unemployment is greatest among unskilled workers, although the restrictions in employment caused by high real wage rates are principally in highly skilled, high wage jobs. This apparent anomaly is explained by underemployment. When high real wage rates restrict employment in high-skill occupations, the workers displaced find jobs in medium-skill occupations, displacing workers from there to low-skill occupations, and the persons displaced there become unemployed. If the restrictions at the top were removed, there would be a shuffle up the skill ladder. While the additional people employed would largely be unskilled, the additional jobs created would highly skilled. When employment is reduced by high union wages, it is in unionized occupations and these are concentrated in skilled rather than unskilled trades. The effect on output and GNP depends on the productivity of the jobs done, not on the skill level of the people newly employed. Those who were underemployed also become more productive because they make greater use of their skills.

The marginal product of labour is lower than the average product in any occupation with a given capital stock. If real wage rates are reduced and employment increased, the productivity of labour falls because more workers have to share the same amount of capital. At the same time, the marginal product of capital increases. Buildings and machinery become more productive when more workers use them. Increased productivity of capital encourages increased investment, which has multiplier effects on the level of employment and the level of GNP. Thus while the immediate impact of increased employment on GNP is geared to the marginal product of labour, the effect on investment could well result in a total increase in GNP by as large a proportion as the increase in employment.

The effect on GNP of a reduced unemployment rate is difficult to estimate precisely. It would be less immediately than it would be after the system adjusted to a different structure of real wage rates. But if high real wage rates achieved by union power are responsible for 2 to 2.5 per cent of our current unemployment rate, then removal of that distortion in the wage structure could well increase GNP by a comparable proportion. When we add the estimates of .3 to .4 per cent of

GNP as the cost of strikes and lock-outs and .2 per cent as deadweight loss, the overall cost to the economy of the current use of union power through the collective bargaining process is in the order of 2.5 to 3 per cent of GNP. In addition there is the social cost of the inequity caused by the exercise of union power by half the population at the expense of the other half. The magnitudes are certainly sufficient to warrant serious consideration of ways to improve the current system.

Identifying imperfections and estimating the costs that they cause do not in themselves indicate how the imperfections can be overcome. To suggest that the problem derives from union power and we should therefore abolish unions would be naïve in the extreme. Such abolition would be both unwise and impossible. It would be unwise because unions do both good and harm and, on balance, we might well be worse off without them than with them. It would be impossible in a democracy in which close to half the labour force is unionized. But there is clear evidence that public opinion is concerned about the visible symptoms of the problem. Carefully designed policies that would overcome the harm caused by union power, while preserving the ability of unions to discharge their useful role, should meet with widespread public support. If such policies can be devised, it should prove politically feasible to implement them.

It is not obvious what these policies should be. We have at our command historical evidence of the nature of the labour market without unions and collective bargaining, though that market existed long ago in different economic conditions. We know the current system. We also have the entire edifice of economic theory that enables us to analyse the properties of alternative structures and specify the properties of an optimum system. Such analysis will be developed in the chapters that follow.

Chapter 2 discusses the nature of human labour, for that is the service sold in the labour market, and identifies the criteria of optimum market performance. Chapter 3 is concerned with the theory of the labour market and the different types of employment contracts that can exist within it. Chapter 4 analyses the system of collective bargaining. Chapter 5 explores the nature of the public interest in the functioning of the labour market and chapter 6 discusses the special nature of the labour market in the public sector. Chapter 7 considers the alternative possible forms of the labour market and identifies the one that best satisfies the criteria of optimality. The final chapter concludes with clear policy recommendations.

CHAPTER TWO

Human Labour, Human Beings, and Economics

Human labour is a factor of production. In a market economy labour services, like anything else of value, can be bought and sold. Economists can analyse the labour market in the same way as other markets. In his capacity as worker, the human being is a stock of human capital that can yield a flow of labour services. The acquisition of skill is investment in human capital and is comparable with investment in physical capital. The employment contract can be viewed as either the sale of a specified flow of services or the leasing of a unit of human capital. In fact, economists grounded in the theory of markets are inclined to ask what is special about labour.

The unique features of the labour market derive from the inseparability of labour from the labourer. Human labour is the productive activity of a human being, and the human being is the purpose as well as the means of production. If we ignore the humanity of the worker, there is nothing to distinguish the labour market from other markets. Slaves could be bred, trained, sold, and leased in exactly the same ways as animals or machines. It is our respect for the humanity of the worker that imposes special and severe constraints on the working of the labour market and endows the outcome of the market process with special significance. These unique features are worth listing at the outset, for they are the source of the problems that will concern us throughout this study. Until these problems are clearly understood, the search for solutions is futile.

The principal unique feature of labour is that the human capital embodied in the individual cannot itself be owned or controlled by another person. Our fundamental principles of individual freedom prohibit slavery as either a permanent status or a binding indenture for a defined term. Whatever contract of employment the individual may agree to as worker, he remains free to terminate it at will. The few exceptions to this principle, such as the soldier who relinquishes his right to resign when he signs on for a defined term, do not apply to the labour markets with which this study is concerned. While designed to protect the freedom of the individual, the principle that the law will not recognize or enforce a binding contract of service restricts the individual's freedom to exploit his human capital through contract. He owns a valuable block of capital, but he cannot sell shares in it nor can he pledge himself as collateral for a loan. The law that protects his freedom also requires him to be the sole proprietor of himself. His only opportunity in contract is to sell the flow of labour services that derive from his human capital. He cannot sell himself or pledge himself, he can only lease himself and must reserve the right to break any lease.

The principle of self-proprietorship of human capital gives rise to many problems in the labour market that are readily solved for other forms of capital by the process of contract.[1] Birth itself is not appropriately viewed as economic activity, though the birth rate may respond to economic conditions, but birth alone does not give rise to the human capital that is important in the modern world. To be productive, the individual must be educated and trained. Investment in human capital is expensive. At the outset of his life the individual owns nothing but his body and cannot finance his own education. Nor can he acquire education at another's expense in exchange for rights over the ensuing human capital, for such rights cannot be assigned. Loans to finance education and training may be backed by a promise to repay, but they cannot be secured by human capital as collateral. Human capital is accordingly not produced by a market process that relies on the same economic principles that govern the production of physical capital. Human capital is financed either by charity from parents or philanthropic institutions, transfer payments from the state, loans that would otherwise be so weakly secured that governments often assume the role of guarantor, or by employers who must secure their continuing interest in the resulting human capital by indirect means that deter labour mobility.

Since the self-proprietor of human capital cannot commit himself to a long-term employment contract, he is restricted either to instantaneous employment contracts or to more secure employment in which the promise of future remuneration is exchanged for consideration other than indenture. Such consideration typically takes the form of deferred compensation that is sacrificed if the individual exercises his right to withdraw from employment. This process of hedging the inherent uncertainty of the instantaneous labour market is one that will be of concern throughout this study.

The second special feature of the labour market is that the individual human being and the unit of human capital are uniquely associated in society. A person is identified by his occupation in terms both of status and income. The total dependence of the individual on his income from employment means that his interests as a member of society are dominated by his concern for the labour market for his particular skills. The conditions of his employment determine his absolute income and his income relative to others and mark his status in society. Persons with like skills in like occupations are perceived as members of a group. They constitute a class in the sense that members of society are classified by their occupations and incomes. Having like interests and like concerns, members of an occupational class associate together and behave as a group in the exercise of both their economic and political rights. The self-proprietorship of human capital that is the bulwark of individual freedom becomes the identifying characteristic that leads the individual to submerge his individuality in membership of a group. Absolute and relative wages of groups become the central focus of concern about the whole structure of society.

The third distinguishing feature of the labour market is that it is dominated by considerations of equity. Concern for fairness arises in many other cases of economic activity and was central to the concept of the "just price" when attention was focused on exchange of the products of different types of labour. Interest in the "just price" of products waned when the development of free markets resulted in the achievement of equilibrium prices,[2] though regulation of prices in the interest of equity continues when the equilibrium price is considered inequitable. Concern over the "just wage" has grown, however, for the bulk of the populace has become dependent on wages rather than self-employment, the functioning of the labour market has been constrained by the principle of self-proprietorship of human capital, and group behaviour has led to labour markets that are far from perfectly competitive. Today the relative status and the relative incomes of different members of society are so closely related to the labour market that our concern for equity has become focused on the equitable determination of relative wages. Arguments in favour of "equal pay for equal work," and more recently of "equal pay for work of equal value," are current manifestations of the old idea of the " just price" or "just wage."

There is widespread concern in society today about the way in which the labour market functions and the outcome it achieves. The deficiencies of the market process can be examined in relation to three criteria: efficiency, equity, and integrity. The first two have received much attention, the third less than it deserves. Any proposed improvement in the system must be justified by the expectation that it will satisfy these criteria to a greater extent. The next section examines what those criteria really mean.

THE CRITERIA OF LABOUR MARKET PERFORMANCE

Efficiency

The economist's concept of efficiency, and the most valuable one for our purposes, is that associated with the concept of *paretian optimality*. An economic system is efficient if it yields a *paretian optimum*, which is an outcome such that no other possible organization of the economy could result in one person being in a preferred position unless someone else were made worse off. There are in principle an infinite number of *paretian optima*, and a correspondingly infinite number of efficient organizations of the economy, for if one optimum is achieved, it would always be possible to make one person better off and another worse off in such way as to yield a different optimum. Optima are distinguished by the distribution of the benefits of economic activity and that is the issue of equity. Efficiency alone is not a sufficient condition for an economic system to be satisfactory, for some efficient solutions might be grossly inequitable. A society in which a dictator controls everything and owns everyone else as a slave might be efficient but totally unacceptable. It is, of course, because efficiency is not sufficient that we also have the criterion of equity. Although not sufficient, efficiency is nevertheless a necessary condition of an optimum system.

If the system is not efficient in the *paretian* sense, then it would be possible to change it so that one person becomes better off and nobody worse off. That change would be a *paretian* improvement. The new position would be superior to the old in the *paretian* sense and would be more efficient then the old. The criterion of efficiency captures our objective of searching for all possible ways to effect such improvements. An efficient labour market has a number of identifiable characteristics. These are worth discussing because whenever we can recognize a situation in which one or more of these characteristics is not present, we have potential scope for improvement.

Labour is a valuable resource because it can produce goods and services that people want. When human needs and desires remain that could be satisfied by the application of labour, but are not currently being satisfied, then labour is scarce. An efficient labour market would not waste a valuable scarce resource. Thus the first characteristic of an efficient labour market is that labour is fully utilized. This, of course, does not mean that every person should work twenty-four hours a day, or even the maximum number of hours physically possible, because time devoted to leisure also satisfies human desires. Nor does it mean that a short period of unemployment between jobs is wasteful when the worker is efficiently engaged in the search process, for a small inventory of unemployed workers and unfilled jobs is necessary for the market to function. But it does mean that no worker should be idle when he would prefer to work for remuneration that some employer would be willing to pay. If an otherwise idle person were to undertake a task that produced some good or service that someone valued at more than enough to compensate the worker for performing the task, both would be better off and there would be an improvement in efficiency. This characteristic of the full utilization of labour is closely related to the idea of full employment, but the latter term has become so associated with particular statistical measures in a particular institutional setting that it is better to avoid it in this critical analysis of the labour market.

In a modern economy there are many different tasks to be performed and labour must be allocated among them. Some of these tasks produce goods, others perform services, some are in the private sector, and others in the public sector. The allocation of labour is efficient when there is no further opportunity to transfer a worker from one job to another in such way that those who benefit from the new job would be more than willing to compensate those who benefit from the old job for the loss of the worker and the worker himself for any reluctance he might have to change his job. In a perfectly efficient system no worker could find a more valuable job in that sense.

Each worker will naturally tend to choose the job where the willingness to pay for his work is greatest. The market will generate incentives for workers to allocate themselves optimally among jobs if willingness to pay wages always reflects the value of the job done. When the consumer hires the worker directly, he will be willing to pay wages up to a maximum equal to the value to him of having the job performed. When the employer is a firm, its willingness to pay the worker reflects its customers' willingness to pay for the product. Under conditions of perfect competition the firm cannot influence either the wage rate of labour or the selling price of the product. It would therefore be willing to pay wages equal to the selling price of the worker's addition to the output of the firm. With imperfect competition, however, the firm's maximum willingness to pay wages may be less than the customer's willingness to pay for the product if the firm believes that selling additional output will force a price reduction on its entire output, or if additional employment will necessitate a wage increase for all its workers.[3] When the employer is government, its willingness to pay the worker indirectly reflects the taxpayers' willingness to pay to have the job done, though the public sector is in practice far from perfect in its reflection of the desires of taxpayers. While in theory perfect markets work perfectly, in practice employers in both the private and public sectors may be wiling to pay wages that do not perfectly reflect the willingness of customers and taxpayers to pay. The incentives of relative wage offers may then induce workers to allocate themselves inefficiently among jobs.

While the worker may be hired for wages, he remains in control of his own person. The extent to which he is directed by his employer varies among jobs. He must sacrifice some independence of action, for the job involves duties that must be performed, but there is always some extent to which the worker decides how well and how hard he works. In a perfectly efficient labour market there would be no possibility for a worker to adjust his effort in such way that the employer who enjoyed or suffered the consequences would be willing to compensate the worker for the adjustment. This is the criterion by which the incentives inherent in different systems of remuneration must be judged. Time rates, piece rates, bonuses, profit-sharing schemes, and promotion prospects are all ways in which attempts are made to achieve this characteristic of efficiency.

If perfect efficiency in utilization, allocation, and intensity were ever achieved, the structure would rapidly become out of date. In a changing world, existing jobs become obsolete and new jobs arise, the demand for some tasks grows and for others declines. There is a continuous flow of new entrants to the labour force who must be allocated among occupations, and their skills and interests may not match those of people leaving the labour force. An efficient labour market must be capable of adjustment to changes in the demand for jobs and in the supply of workers with different skills. The structure of the labour market will change automatically as jobs become vacant through retirement or death and new entrants are allocated to jobs. But such demographic turnover may be too slow for the system to adjust optimally to changing circumstances. It might be efficient to reallocate an existing worker to a different job and we must consider the characteristics of an efficient degree of job mobility.

When a worker moves from one job to another many persons may be affected. The worker experiences a change in his activities and perhaps his income, the old employer loses the services of the worker and the obligation to pay wages, while the new employer acquires both the services and the obligations. The effects on employers may, in turn, have consequences for their customers and other workers. In the strict *paretian* sense the change is an improvement if at least one person benefits from the change while none suffers from it. A *paretian* improvement is not necessarily equitable if all the benefit accrues to one person rather than being shared, especially if the person receiving the benefit is not considered to deserve it. Moreover, some changes that are not *paretian* improvements may nevertheless be welfare improvements if deserving parties gain significantly while less deserving parties suffer insignificantly. The extent to which mobility is a good thing is a complex question.

If the labour market were perfect and there were no costs associated with labour mobility, a maximum degree of mobility would be efficient. Workers would move from job to job on a day to day basis in response to the slightest incentive. In practice, however, mobility does impose costs on both employer and employee. No two jobs are identical and a new worker is not fully effective until he has learned the job. The learning process sometimes involves extensive on-the-job training, but it always involves acquiring familiarity with the procedures of the job, the layout of the workplace, and the personalities and practices of those with whom the new employee must work. The employer inevitably bears the costs of low initial productivity during the learning process. The employee also bears some of the costs of adjustment. These may be high if, for example, he has to relocate his home and family, or low if he only has to learn such simple things as the best route to work and the best place to lunch. If the labour market were perfectly flexible, one party could impose inefficiently high mobility costs on another and there would be an inefficiently high degree of mobility. This possibility is readily illustrated by a simple example.

Firm A currently employs worker X, firm B has a job vacant, and worker Y enters the labour force. Either Y works for B, or Y works for A and X moves to B. With perfect flexibility, firm A may hire Y and dismiss X in response to some slight apparent advantage, thereby forcing X to incur perhaps substantial costs of moving to B. Alternatively X may take the initiative and move from A to B for a slight gain, leaving A to incur the costs of hiring and training Y. In either event one party has imposed inefficiently high costs on another. Such an inefficiently high degree of mobility can be avoided by forcing each party to bear the costs of its own decisions. If A had to compensate X fully, by severance pay, for example, A would not change workers. If X had to compensate A fully, by loss of seniority pay or pension rights, for example, X would not move. But if such compensation is excessive, it would deter efficient reallocation of labour as well as inefficient. Provisions for severance pay and benefits of seniority create frictions in the process of labour reallocation. An efficient labour market has the right degree of friction. Too little or too much friction is inefficient.

The matching of workers to jobs requires much information. Information is not a free good, its acquisition involves often substantial search costs and takes time. A firm with a job vacancy takes time and incurs costs to find the right employee, and the worker without a job takes time and incurs costs to find one. An efficient market economizes in the use of any costly input, and information is no exception. Since search costs are involved every time an employment contract terminates, efficiency requires employment contracts that continue for some time, and the higher the search costs, the longer the efficient term of the contract.[4] If an employment contract can be terminated at any time by one party, the other continuously bears the risk of having to incur search costs. Risk is itself a cost that individuals are prepared to pay to avoid. Thus efficiency requires some security in the contract of employment for both parties.

The labour market is asymmetric in its ability to secure contracts of employment. The employer can guarantee employment for a defined period or for life, but the employee cannot bind himself to an enforceable indenture. The solution to this problem has been to devise enforceable forms of liquidated damages, that is, compensation that will be paid by the defaulting party to the other, the extent of which is agreed as part of the contract. The employer who terminates employment may have to pay severance compensation, while the employee who terminates may sacrifice pension rights and lose seniority. In addition, both parties may carry insurance, the employer on the life of an employee whose death would cause substantial costs, and the employee in the form of unemployment insurance.

Such costs, like the adjustment costs previously discussed, mean that it is efficient for the labour market to tie employees to employers. If those ties are too weak, the system incurs inefficiently high search costs, but if they are too strong, the system is prevented from adjusting efficiently to changing circumstances that call for some reallocation of labour.

The problem with any long-term contract is to specify its terms. When the contract is made there can never be perfect foresight and there is accordingly need for periodic restatement of the terms of a continuing contract. While any term or condition of the contract may be revised, the wage rate is the most commonly contentious issue. Economic conditions change substantially during the life of a worker in ways that can never be fully anticipated. Money wage rates become obsolete with inflation, and wage rates tied to the consumer price index or other economic indices can never anticipate changes in the relative equilibrium wage rates of different occupations. Thus the paradoxical situation arises that both parties are committed to continuation of a contract of employment, with liquidated damages for noncompliance, while the terms of the continuing contract to which they are bound are not specified. Resolution of that paradox involves costs, and an efficient labour market minimizes those costs.

Negotiation of the future terms of a continuing contract involves costs of negotiation. Breakdown of the negotiations can involve very high costs of strike and lock-out, the incidence of which falls partly on the employer, partly on the employee, and partly on third parties who are consumers of the product or suppliers of complementary factors of production. If new terms are imposed by either party, by arbitration or by legislation, there may be costs of resentment. Persons who feel aggrieved by a perceived injustice suffer a loss of utility. Resentment and demoralization may lead to a loss of productivity.

Disputes can be resolved in two ways when the parties fail to reach agreement. One route begins with the premise that the contentious item has never been agreed. Workers and employers are presumed to have committed themselves to continuing employment at a wage rate to be determined or revised later. The problem then is to determine a "fair" wage, and appeal is made to the criterion of equity. The other route begins with the premise that there was agreement, though one or other party may regret having agreed in the light of subsequent changes in economic conditions. The problem then is to enforce the agreement that was once voluntarily made, for a deal is a deal, and appeal is made to the criterion of integrity.

Equity

Any voluntary contract yields benefits to both parties, for otherwise they would not voluntarily make it. Economists call the net benefit rent, which can be defined as the excess of what a person derives from a contract over the minimum that would persuade him to agree to it. Thus the rent derives from the opportunity to enter into a favourable contract. More generally, rent can be defined as the difference between the benefits derived from two situations, or as the net benefit yielded by the opportunity to move from one situation to another. The concept of rent can be applied to a pair of situations that differ only slightly or greatly. The rent from employment in one firm rather than a comparable job in another may be small, while the rent from employment in one of the professions rather than the opportunities that would have been available with no postsecondary education may be very large. At the macro level, all members of society derive rents from the opportunity to participate in the economic system by comparison with what their circumstances would be if there were a total breakdown of the economy. Equity is fairness in the distribution of rents. Just as the concept of rent can be applied to many comparisons of different circumstances, so can the concept of equity.

Horizontal Equity The most commonly proposed principle of equity, often referred to as horizontal equity, is the equal treatment of equals. The problem with this principle is that in its strict sense it is tautological and in any other sense ambiguous. Two persons who are exactly equal in all respects must always be treated equally because there is no difference by which to distinguish them. The principle that people who are equal in all *relevant* respects should be treated equally begs the question of what is relevant. The less that is considered relevant, the broader is the application of the principle. In the extreme case, only humanity is relevant and the principle then argues for total egalitarianism. A few examples will illustrate the problem of defining what is relevant.

Should two workers who perform identical tasks in the same workplace be paid the same wage rate? Today it is accepted that any difference of race or sex between them is irrelevant, but that principle was not always commonly held. It may be argued that any difference of age is irrelevant, but it is not generally agreed that any difference of seniority is irrelevant. Two school teachers, for example, who teach the same subjects to children of the same age may be paid different wages if one has been doing so for twenty years and the other for two, although there may be no evidence that the senior person is the better teacher. There is no inequity when workers accept employment knowing that the wage will rise with years of service. In other cases, differences in wage rates may reflect differences in the nature of the employment contract. One worker, for example, may have long-term security of employment and a lower wage rate, while another is hired for only a short time at a higher wage. Consultants employed for a specific assignment of short duration are often paid more than comparably qualified permanent staff. There can be no inequity if all workers have the same options and face the same trade-off between wages and security. Horizontal equity is violated only if equally qualified workers are remunerated differently under otherwise identical contracts, for one is then given an option the other is denied.

Should two workers who perform similar tasks in different workplaces be paid the same wage rate? Should the man who bolts the wheels on agricultural machinery be paid the same as the man who bolts the wheels on new cars? Should the man who works in a factory in Halifax be paid the same wage as the man who does a similar job in Toronto? In practice there are significant differences in wage rates for the same job among different firms, different industries, and different locations.

Should two workers who perform different tasks be paid the same wage if the jobs are similar in their requirements of skill, effort, responsibility, and working conditions? This is the principle of equal pay for work of equal value. In practice, of course, members of different professions may earn very different incomes even though their qualifications are comparable. Such differences may similarly arise within a single profession when the specialisms are different. A professor of classics in a university may receive a different salary from that of a comparably qualified engineer or accountant.

The differences that arise in practice in such cases typically reflect the differences of market pressures and there has never been reason to suppose that markets work equitably. In each segment of the labour market there is at any time a certain supply of workers with the appropriate attributes and a certain demand for their services. For differences in wage rates to arise and persist two things must be true: workers with different wage rates must not be perfectly substitutable in the work process, for otherwise demand would switch from the higher paid group to the lower paid; and workers must be unable freely and costlessly to change their relevant attributes, for otherwise supply would shift from the lower paid group to the higher paid. Given these conditions, wage differences perform two very important functions in the labour market. Differential wage rates encourage employment of the group in high supply relative to demand and encourage economy in the use of those in low supply relative to demand. With perfectly competitive markets and perfectly flexible wages, the result would be full employment for all with no critical areas of labour shortage. The second function is to encourage workers to move into the higher paid occupations and locations. This is particularly important for new entrants to the labour force, especially young workers, who have not yet committed themselves to particular skills. Differential wages are the market's way to channel workers into the occupations and locations where their work is most highly valued.

If our concern for equity led us to enforce equal wages despite any of the differences mentioned above, then we should either have to find some other mechanism to perform the rationing and allocation functions, or suffer the consequences of having no such mechanism. We could, of course, plan such matters by directives – rationing workers in short supply and refusing permission for an employer to hire such persons to an extent greater than that considered appropriate to our social priorities, and directing existing workers to move to, and new workers to enter, those occupations where they are considered most essential. Such measures are used in wartime when the composition of the needed labour force is so different from that existing in peacetime that mere wage differentials would not suffice to bring about the transition fast enough. But in normal circumstances our society would consider direction of the labour force to be more intolerable as an infringement of personal liberty than are wage differentials as an infringement of equity. If wages are constrained to equality, with no other mechanism of rationing and allocation, the consequences would be shortage of those workers whose market wage would be higher and unemployment for those whose wages would be lower without such constraint. Those fortunate enough to secure workers of the scarce variety would have no incentive to employ them efficiently, and the potential work of those unemployed would be wasted. Concern for both equity and freedom would then conflict with the desire for efficiency.

In practice our society does not enforce equal wages, but it does severely limit the extent to which wages may be unequal. Minimum wage laws that impose a lower limit on the wage rate for any occupational group inevitably cause unemployment among workers whose wages would otherwise be lower. The progressive income tax results in smaller differences in post-tax incomes than exist in pre-tax incomes. This does not detract from the rationing function of wage differentials because employers are guided by the gross wage rates they must pay. But it does detract from the allocation function, for the smaller the difference in post-tax income received by the worker, the weaker the incentive to move to a higher paid occupation.

If wage differentials guide the allocation of labour, then differential unemployment rates can similarly be expected to do so. If the young entrant to the labour force is motivated to enter a high wage rather than a low wage occupation, then he should be motivated to enter an occupation where there is full employment rather than one where there is high unemployment. That motive is, of course, weaker the more generous the transfer payments to the unemployed.[5] There is an important difference, however, between the choice of occupations that lead to different wages with some certainty, and the choice when the wage rates are less unequal and unemployment for the individual is a matter of uncertainty. Optimists will expect to be lucky in getting a job. For them differential unemployment rates constitute a less powerful incentive than wage differentials. For pessimists and those who dislike risks – the risk averse – differential prospects of unemployment will be a stronger motive for occupational choice than different wage rates.

Economic analysis based on comparison of static equilibria would argue that either differential wages or differential unemployment rates constitute an incentive to labour mobility so that in either case the long-run equilibrium is one of full employment with equal wage rates. But in practice long-run static equilibrium is never achieved. The relative demands for workers of different types change continuously and supplies are slow to adjust. We are always in the adjustment process. Some changes in demand are long-term, others are short-term fluctuations. The changes are long-term when the decline in demand in one occupation and increase in another will last long enough to justify the mobility costs involved in reallocating the labour force. Short-term fluctuations are the consequence of volatile product market conditions and do not persist long enough to justify reallocation.

When reallocation is called for, wage differentials that achieve full employment are continuously more efficient as an incentive to optimal allocation of labour than are differences in unemployment rates, for in the former case some workers earn less than an equitable amount, but they do work, while in the latter case some earn nothing while unemployed, and their labour is wasted. It may be argued that wage differentials are inequitable, but it is not clear that they are more inequitable than differential probabilities of being unemployed. Either process of generating incentives to encourage efficient allocation of labour involves some inequity in the interest of efficiency.

Differences in employment, or unemployment, may, however, be more efficient than wage differences in the case of short-term fluctuations. In a particular month one firm may experience low sales while another faces excess orders. The former may temporarily lay off workers while the latter works overtime. If all markets were instantly responsive and mobility totally costless, the wage rate would fall in the former firm, rise in the latter, and workers move from one to the other. But when movement is not costless and the apparent imbalance is temporary, such adjustments may not be worthwhile. If the imbalance is of short enough duration in relation to mobility costs, it would be more efficient for the former firm's workers to suffer temporary lay-off while the latter work overtime, with no adjustment in wage rates. In an extreme example, we do not find the sales clerk in a clothing store being offered lower wages whenever there is no customer in the store, nor do we find him resigning and accepting employment in the furniture store next door because a customer there is awaiting attention. Adjustments do take place more readily in the casual labour market where the cost of mobility is low. Babysitters, for example, serve whatever employer demands their services on a particular evening, but even in this case the wage rate adjusts to temporary demand changes only on extreme occasions such as New Year's Eve.

A second reason why extreme flexibility of wage rates may be inefficient arises with the macrodynamics of fluctuations. No economy is ever in perfect static equilibrium. Demand fluctuates in temporary booms and slumps. If wage rates adjusted instantly to changing demand, a temporary downturn would cause lower wages, lower incomes, and lower demand. A minor hiatus in demand could snowball into a recession. A temporary spurt in demand could similarly trigger an inflationary spiral. Some inflexibility of wage rates may serve to stabilize the economic system as a whole.

A third case in which some unemployment may be more efficient than wage changes arises when labour markets are not perfectly competitive, wage rates are negotiated, and employers have better information about market conditions than workers. Employers may then be tempted to exaggerate adverse product market conditions if they could use such false argument to achieve lower wage rates, but would have no incentive to exaggerate if wages were inflexible and they could only reduce employment and output. The inherent inefficiency of changes in employment rather than wage rates may then be a cost worth paying in the interest of greater honesty in negotiation.

Despite the arguments for some short-term inflexibility of wage rates, it remains true that unemployment involves the loss of labour services while wage changes do not. From the standpoint of horizontal equity, a fall in the wage rate for all workers in an occupation is less inequitable than unemployment for some. There may well be situations in which some short-term unemployment is the lesser evil, but such cases are exceptions to the general rule that wage differences are both more efficient and more equitable than differences in unemployment rates as a mechanism to guide the allocation of labour.

Vertical Equity The second principle of equity, often referred to as vertical equity, is that workers who differ in relevant ways should be paid appropriately different wages. Differences in the ability, skill, or effort of different workers and differences in the unpleasantness, danger, or responsibility associated with different jobs should be reflected in appropriately different rewards. Specification of the appropriate wage differences involves issues of efficiency and equity. If some workers are to undertake unpleasant, dangerous, or arduous tasks, they must be encouraged to do so voluntarily by adequate incentives. The costs of acquiring needed skills will be incurred only if there is prospect of adequate return. Workers with great ability or high levels of skill are very valuable to society and high wages encourage employers to economize in their employment. Equity suggests that workers who choose to become more productive, or undertake less attractive tasks, deserve greater reward than those who do not. If all workers were free to qualify for and to enter all occupations, then the wage differentials required for efficiency would also be equitable. No person could claim unfair treatment by comparison with another if he had the option of changing places.

In practice workers do not have total freedom of choice, or complete equality of opportunity, and efficient differentials are not necessarily equitable. Some persons have native abilities others do not possess. Some of those abilities lead to high productivity and would result in high efficient wage rates. The principles of personal freedom and self-proprietorship of human capital suggest that individuals should receive the fruits of their own native abilities, but a compassionate society tempers the consequences of disabilities. Our sense of equity suggests that wage differentials attributable to differences in native ability should be smaller than the consequent differences in productivity. One solution is to design a system of progressive taxes and transfers that leave gross wage rates to be dictated by considerations of efficiency while net incomes are dictated by equity. Such a system does not detract from efficient choice by the individual in the case of native ability, for native abilities cannot be chosen.

Some individuals have wider freedom of choice than others to acquire education and training. The children of well-educated, high income families typically have greater opportunities for advanced education. In this case, efficiency and equity cannot be fully reconciled by progressive taxation. Consider four persons, A, B, C, and D. A and B had the opportunity to acquire human capital. A did so but B declined. C and D did not have the opportunity. If they had, C would have acquired the skill but D would not. A is the only one with the acquired skill and efficiency requires that his wage rate be higher than the others'. There is no reason in equity to transfer income from A to B, for B had the opportunity but declined it. Nor is there reason to distinguish B and D. As neither would have chosen to acquire the skill, the absence of opportunity for D is irrelevant to the outcome, though D may well feel aggrieved at having been denied the opportunity to choose for himself. C, however, is unfairly treated in comparison with A, for C would have chosen A's situation if he had the chance. Yet there is no way to distinguish B, C, and D by a progressive tax system, nor does the principle of horizontal equity suggest that they should be distinguished. In this case the use of progressive taxation to achieve smaller post-tax income differences than the pre-tax wage differential required to induce efficient use of labour will at best be a compromise among the appropriate treatment of B, C, and D. The more C is compensated on grounds of equity, the more is efficient incentive upset between A and B. The only full solution in such a case is to ensure that C and D do have opportunities comparable with A and B.

A further reason to narrow wage differentials by progressive taxation arises when the acquisition of human capital is subsidized. Efficiency requires that skill should be acquired whenever the increase in productivity more than compensates for the cost of training. If each individual were free to choose and bore the full cost of his own training, incentives would be both efficient and equitable with efficient wage differentials. But the principle of self-proprietorship of human capital makes it impossible for individuals to choose to finance their own training. When education and training are subsidized by the state, the cost to the individual is reduced. Unless the post-tax reward for the skill acquired is reduced comparably, there would be excessive incentive to acquire skill, which would violate the principle of efficiency. Since the skilled person would receive the full wage differential, while taxpayers paid part of the cost of his training, equity would also be violated.

An efficient labour market must determine for different types of labour the differential wage rates that will encourage their efficient employment. But receipt of such differentials by workers would in many cases violate the principles of equity. Post-tax wage differentials can be reduced by progressive taxation, but it is not possible to apply different tax structures to wage differentials that arise for different reasons, although such distinctions would be appropriate on grounds of equity. Whatever the compromise tax system employed, there will be grounds in equity for further *ad hoc* adjustment, and to the extent that the tax system violates efficient incentives, there will also be grounds in efficiency for *ad hoc* adjustments.

Thus we cannot rely on labour markets to satisfy fully and automatically both the criteria of efficiency and equity. Progressive taxation might achieve a better outcome than would exist without it, but it cannot be applied selectively to meet the requirements of both efficiency and equity. Further refinement, if it is to be selective, must be on an *ad hoc* basis and with no clearly defined principles of equity it becomes arbitrary. Even if the principles of equity were precisely defined, the absence of full information would preclude determination of wages by a preset formula and the process would still be arbitrary. It is little wonder that the search for both efficiency and equity has led to the widespread use of arbitration with no clearly defined principles to guide the arbitrator.

Wage differentials create incentives that guide the allocation of labour. Workers are influenced by relative wages in their choices of careers and occupations. But the choice of career precedes the receipt of wages, and the choice becomes more binding the higher the costs of mobility. Thus the worker is guided by his expectation of the wage differentials that will prevail many years in the future, and the future is uncertain. In the pure model of self-proprietorship of human capital the individual worker bears the uncertainty. He acquires skills and commits himself to an occupation on the basis of his own prediction of future wage rates. He has no redress if his expectations are not realized.

The individual can be relieved of uncertainty in two ways. Employers can specify future wage rates and guarantee long-term employment, with liquidated damages for noncompliance. This shifts the burden of uncertainty from the employee to the employer. Society as a whole can stipulate in advance the structure of taxation and the principles of equity enshrined in law. This removes uncertainty about the future from the shoulders of individuals but at the expense of constraining the flexibility of future policy. The individual then makes his choices not simply on the basis of his own predictions, but on the basis of explicit promises. To the extent that promises are made and wages specified in advance, such promises should be kept. This is the principle of integrity.

Integrity

Integrity is the essence of the law of contract. A contract is the exchange of promises between two parties by which they are bound in law. Contracts and their enforcement are the essential mechanism by which the interdependence relationships of an exchange economy are arranged. If a contract is precisely specified, redress can be sought in the courts by either party if the other defaults. In a contract of employment the employee promises to perform certain tasks, or such tasks as may be assigned by management within a defined range, in exchange for remuneration in the form of money wages and various other benefits. Employment contracts are severely constrained by the extent to which the employee can be required to honour a promise to work. He cannot sell himself into slavery or a long-term indenture. The form of redress for breach of contract is in practice limited to monetary damages, which in turn are limited by the defendant's ability to pay.

TYPES OF EMPLOYMENT
CONTRACTS

While the possible variety of employment contracts is virtually unlimited, they can for analytical purposes be grouped into three types. The first is of very short duration, often called casual labour, the second continues for a significant defined period of time, and the third continues indefinitely. Contracts in which the unit of work is a specified task rather than work for a unit of time fall into similar categories and need not be treated separately.

The first type of contract, which we shall call the spot labour market, causes no problem of integrity. The worker is hired for a very short period, or a small defined task, and is not paid until the end of the period or completion of the task. The worker can, if necessary, sue for payment and the employer withholds payment until the job is completed. Since it is fully specified and voluntary by both parties, the contract itself cannot inflict inequity on either party. Any attempt to impose wage rates or conditions of employment on grounds of equity different from those determined by market forces will result in either a shortage of labour or unemployment. The problem with this type of contract is that when the work is of a continuing nature the necessity to arrange new contracts on a daily basis gives rise to inefficiently high search and mobility costs, and exposes both parties to uncertainty concerning the availability of jobs and workers. It is because of these inefficiencies that there is recourse to other types of contract, though the spot labour market remains important for tasks of a casual or intermittent kind.

The contract for a defined period again gives rise to no problem of integrity or equity, for the terms of employment can be clearly specified in advance and both parties agree that the contract terminates on a defined date. If the employer defaults in payment, the worker can sue. If the worker fails to perform his duties, he can be dismissed. The worker has security of employment and income for the life of the contract, but the employer's security is limited and relies on deterrents. There can be no guarantee that the worker will not become ill or die during the contract, but he is deterred from leaving voluntarily by the difficulty of finding alternative employment in mid-season, if the work is of a seasonal nature, by the implicit threat of bad references that will hurt his future employment prospects, or by the withholding of terminal compensation. If the contract is for a long period, the agreed wage rate may increase during the life of the contract. When the contract specifies an increasing schedule of wages, the higher wages late in the contract may be deferred compensation that is sacrificed if the worker leaves during the life of the contract. Such sacrifice serves as liquidated damages for failure of the employee to complete the agreed period of employment.

The defined period contract does give rise to problems of efficiency when the work to be performed continues beyond the life of the contract. Such contracts are most appropriate for discrete or seasonal tasks. Construction workers may be hired for the duration of a particular project, since the employer wishes to avoid the uncertainties of the spot market while the work is in progress, but does not wish to incur continuing obligations when the project is completed. Agricultural workers may be hired for a single harvest season and teachers for a single school year. But when the work is continuous and expected to continue indefinitely, the use of defined period employment contracts leaves both parties with the need periodically to arrange new contracts. Either a new contract will be arranged between the previous parties or both will incur costs of search and mobility. Specifying the terms of a renewed contract involves negotiation costs. Since failure to agree would involve search costs for both parties, both have an incentive to agree, but each can exploit the potential costs that failure to agree would impose on the other by holding out for favourable terms. The highest wage the employer would pay rather than find another worker will exceed the minimum the worker would accept rather than find another job, the difference being geared to their combined costs of search, training, and mobility. If the difference is significant, the negotiation costs can be high. There is no way in which market forces can determined the outcome within the defined range, for there are only two parties in the particular market. The expected willingness of other employers to hire the worker and of other workers to accept employment determine the expected search costs and the range of possible agreement, but cannot define the outcome within that range. The outcome depends upon the relative bargaining strength of the parties, which reflects the costs incurred by each if there is failure to agree.

Arrangement of continuing employment by a series of defined period contracts raises the issue of the optimum length of the contract period. Short periods mean frequent renegotiation, high negotiation costs, and high costs of uncertainty about whether a favourable subsequent contract can be arranged. But long contracts commit the parties well into the future to terms that they may come to regret. The security of a long-term contract may be asymmetric. The employer may be bound to pay specified wages for the life of the contract if the worker continues to be willing to perform the specified work. The employee's security is restricted only by the potential bankruptcy of the employer. But the employee is bound only by such liquidated damages as may be built into the contract. Loss of seniority or pension rights may be a powerful deterrent to the employee's withdrawal during the contract, but is unlikely to afford the employer as much security of continuing service by the worker as the worker has security of income. Since the worker cannot guarantee to continue to work, the employer may exchange the security of a long period contract only for a lower wage rate. The length of the contract then becomes one of the items to be negotiated.

Whatever the terms specified at the outset of a defined period contract, there is no problem of integrity if those terms are enforced. Failure to agree on the terms of a subsequent contract leaves neither party with any obligation to the other. The issues of equity surround the terms agreed at the outset and agreement obviates the need for arbitration or imposed equity. The only problem with such contracts concerns the efficiency costs of periodic renegotiation or search and mobility.

In the process of negotiating the length of a defined period contract, each party wishes to commit the other but each wishes to retain flexibility. The security of the contract for each party is only as great as the enforceable or liquidated damages for default by the other. If the extent of such damages is agreed, it may then be unnecessary to specify the length of the defined period. The contract of employment may continue until one party terminates it and pays the liquidated damages. Dismissal may require specified notice, or payment in lieu thereof,[6] and resignation may involve the loss of accumulated seniority and pension rights. This third type of contract, the indefinite period contract, is perhaps the most common in the labour market.

The indefinite period contract would give rise to no problem of integrity if its terms were clearly specified and honoured. It may be agreed, or at least understood, that the employee will work until death or retirement or until he chooses to resign. Voluntary resignation may involve loss of seniority and pension rights, and because the costs of mobility for the worker may increase with age, the deterrent to withdrawal becomes stronger as time passes. The employer will continue to pay wages and other benefits until he goes out of business or dismisses the employee with appropriate notice or severance settlement. At first the employee has the greater security, for he can claim notice or severance compensation if he is dismissed, while the employer has little deferred compensation to retain if the employee withdraws. With the passage of time, however, the worker becomes less mobile and the prospect of his withdrawing voluntarily falls, while the employer is still bound by the same penalties for dismissal. Security increases more for the employer than it does for the employee.

The major problem with the indefinite period contract in practice is the specification of remuneration. While the initial wage rate can easily be stated in money terms, it is more difficult to state in real terms and it is still more difficult to specify in advance the way in which remuneration will adjust to changing circumstances. Nor can the progress of the employee easily be specified in advance. There may be agreed provision for a wage increase following a period of probation or training, but no specification of promotion rights thereafter. Neither party typically believes that at the beginning of employment there is clear agreement what the wage rate will be ten or twenty years later. Thus both parties find themselves committed to a contract of continuing employment, with liquidated damages for default, but without complete specification of the terms of the contract by which they are bound.

The indefinite period contract is subject to continual renegotiation. In the absence of any agreement to the contrary, either party can initiate negotiation of revised conditions at any time. Continuous uncertainty concerning the future terms of the contract is in the interest of neither party, however. This often leads to agreement that the terms once settled will remain unchanged for a stated period. Wages and other conditions may then be agreed for a one, two, or three year period, with agreement that the contract will then be renegotiated. The indefinite period contract with terms specified for a defined period is quite distinct from the defined period contract. In the defined period contract both parties agree that all obligations to each other expire on the expiry of the defined period. In the indefinite period contract, however, there is the common expectation that employment will continue beyond the period for which the wage rate is agreed. That expectation is reflected in seniority rights, pension plans, and other ways. The employer is not free to negotiate a new contract with some workers and not others at his discretion. Employees typically have rights to continued employment under the new contract, unless they are dismissed for cause. They may similarly have limited rights to compensation from their pension fund if they refuse continued employment. The existence of continuing obligations is the essential feature of the indefinite period contract of employment even though the precise terms of the contract are agreed only for a defined term. An extreme case of such a contract exists in the universities where tenure guarantees the professor continued employment until retirement unless cause for dismissal can be demonstrated, while the remuneration for the employment is renegotiated annually.

The indefinite period contract gives rise to problems of efficiency, equity, and integrity. The efficiency problem concerns the cost of repeated renegotiation of the conditions of the contract. When the parties fail to agree, the achievement of a fair settlement becomes a problem of equity. If the parties do reach agreement, any failure to honour that agreement constitutes a breach of integrity. A serious conflict between equity and integrity arises when conditions that were once agreed are no longer considered fair. There are many examples in which legislation has imposed changes in the conditions of employment in the interests of equity, even though such imposed changes constitute violations of integrity. Employers and employees may agree on a wage rate, only to have it changed by a minimum wage law. They may agree about the liquidated damages that arise if the employer terminates the contract. The employee might, for example, be entitled to a specific period of notice. He might subsequently become entitled by law to sue for more extensive damages for wrongful dismissal. Sacrifice of pension rights as the agreed penalty for termination by the employee may be overridden by compulsory vesting. Agreement that employment will terminate at a defined retirement age may be overridden by prohibition of mandatory retirement.

The principles of property rights and voluntary exchange require a legal system to enforce contracts. The honouring of contracts is the basic principle of integrity. Equity is the specification of fairness for parties who fail to agree. When the principle of equity is used to sanction both failure to enforce agreements previously made and the imposition on either party of obligations never agreed to, then the criteria of equity and integrity are in conflict. The practice of overriding contracts to conform with subsequently held concepts of equity weakens the incentive for the parties to reach agreement carefully on the conditions of indefinite period contracts. There is little point in reaching agreement if there is little faith that the agreement can subsequently be enforced.

Law is made by the political process, while contracts are made by the market process. Once it is believed that the political process can be used to override contracts made by the market process, the attention of the parties is diverted from negotiation in the market to pressure and propaganda in the political arena. When the contract of employment is not clearly specified, disputes cannot be resolved by integrity. If the political process fails to impose a solution, they are not resolved by equity. Failure to resolve a dispute by either means gives rise to serious problems of efficiency.

It is now time to examine the basic economic theory of the market process to ask how it explains the determination of the terms of contracts under various conditions and how far the equilibrium outcomes satisfy the criteria of efficiency, equity, and integrity.

CHAPTER THREE

The Theory of the Labour Market

In economic theory, and particularly the theory of markets, the simplest models that assume away the complexities and obstacles of the real world often work smoothly and achieve equilibria with ideal properties. As complexity is introduced difficulties arise. The analytical process of introducing complexities one at a time permits us to establish which imperfections cause which problems, though some problems result from a combination of causes. Identifying the cause of a problem is the first step toward finding a solution. The labour market can be analysed in this way, the simplest model being the spot market with perfect and costless mobility. The simplest case will be discussed first and then the more complicated ones that give rise to the problems encountered in the real world.

THE SPOT LABOUR MARKET

In a spot market labour is hired for a very short period of time or for a small, defined task. My primary interest is in the forces that determine the wage rate rather than such matters as the length of the working day. I shall accordingly define the unit of labour as a day's work and assume that the length of the working day, or the magnitude of a defined task that constitutes a day's work, is already established by convention. The quantity of labour hired can thus be expressed as a number of workers, which is the appropriate unit for subsequent consideration of labour mobility and the number of people in each occupation. In this way we can avoid the complications of shorter or longer working days, whether workers would want more or less hours of employment at a higher wage rate, and whether an employer hires more people for short days or fewer people for long days. Such questions are, of course, important and they can be analysed by models in which the volume of employment is defined as the number of man hours per week, but as they are not my principal concern, I shall abstract from them in the interest of simplicity.

In the simplest model we can assume that all workers and all jobs are homogeneous in all relevant respects, and that mobility costs and information costs are zero. Any worker is as good as any other as far as the employer is concerned, workers have no preferences among jobs or employers, employers can change workers and workers can change employers without cost to either, and all know perfectly the information concerning the availability of jobs and workers. This is a simple competitive market. The number of potential workers is fixed by the size of the population in the relevant age group. Some potential workers may not consider it worth working at low wage rates, so the supply curve of labour is upward sloping. The demand curve is downward sloping, for some employers will consider some workers worth hiring at low wages but not at high wages, so the number of jobs falls as the wage rate rises. Such a market has a simple, stable equilibrium with a single wage rate. Zero mobility costs and full information make such a market instantly responsive to changing economic circumstances and equilibrium is continuously achieved.

When we relax the simple assumptions of homogeneity and costless mobility, the market breaks down into a number of separate submarkets, each one representing a particular occupation in a particular geographical area. If movement among occupations or areas were impossible, each submarket would have the same characteristics as the single labour market. An equilibrium wage would prevail in each submarket but different submarkets could well have different wage rates. Wage differentials would change as each submarket adjusted separately to changing demand.

The most realistic assumption is that mobility among submarkets is neither costless nor impossible. Mobility is possible but it involves costs of retraining and relocation and it takes time. Any widening of the wage differential between two submarkets will lead to a flow of workers from the low wage occupation to the high wage one. The wider the differential, the greater that flow will be. This adjustment process on the supply side of the market is illustrated in figure 1.

Figure 1

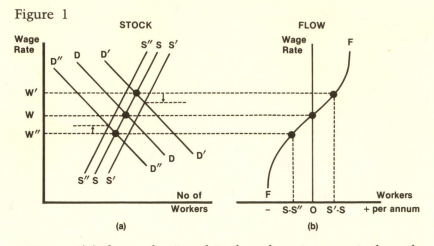

Figure 1(a) shows the "stock" of workers in a particular sub-market at a moment of time as the supply curve ss. Since mobility takes time, the number of potential workers is independent of the wage rate, but the labour supply curve is upward sloping because some individuals may be more willing to work at higher wages. The demand for workers, DD, is downward sloping and the equilibrium wage is w. Figure 1(b) shows the "flow" supply curve FF, which indicates the net number of workers per annum that would flow into (+) or out of (-) the submarket as a function of the wage rate. At wage w, the net flow is zero, retiring workers are just replaced, and the stock of workers in the submarket remains constant. If demand increased to D'D', the wage would increase to w' and there would be a net flow into the submarket of S'-S workers per annum. After one year the stock would have increased to S' and the equilibrium wage would be falling. If there is a reduction of demand to D"D", the wage falls to w", there is a net outflow of workers, the stock falls, and the wage rate begins to rise again.

The degree of mobility into and out of the submarket is captured by the shape of the flow supply curve FF. If mobility is perfect, the flow supply curve is perfectly elastic and FF is a horizontal straight line. The slightest change in the wage rate as a result of a change in demand will cause an immediate inflow or outflow of workers that will bring the wage rate back to equilibrium. If mobility is impossible, FF, is highly inelastic, for the only possible adjustment is in the allocation of new workers among submarkets. If the wage rate increases, the maximum inflow of new workers will be a small proportion of the existing stock and the stock is slow to increase. If the wage rate falls, outflow is possible only by attrition through death or retirement and the maximum outflow is small in relation to the existing stock.

The level of FF, and the wage at which the net flow is zero, will depend on prevailing wage rates in other submarkets. If wages rise elsewhere, there will be a net outflow from the submarket under analysis and the flow supply curve will move vertically upward. A fall in wage rates elsewhere would cause the flow supply curve to fall vertically and there would be a net flow into the submarket under analysis until equilibrium is restored.

The spot labour market, in which the wage rate in each submarket is determined by the free operation of supply and demand, is perfectly efficient if there are no information costs. Any worker who is willing to work for a wage that some employer is prepared to pay will find employment. Employers will hire workers from low wage submarkets in place of those from high wage submarkets to whatever extent is profitable and this will be the efficient extent of substitution. Workers will move among submarkets in response to wage differentials when the differential is sufficient to warrant the costs of mobility. The criterion of integrity is also fully met. Each worker is a self-proprietor of his own human capital and can earn whatever wages some employer is prepared to pay for his services. There are no promises of continuing wages, so no promises are broken.

The spot market, however, does not necessarily satisfy the criterion of equity. There is no problem of equity if mobility is perfect and costless, for all workers are interchangeable and all receive the same wage rate. But when there are mobility costs, wage differentials among submarkets will ensue from changing demands for labour although workers are still equal in ability, skill, and effort. The workers are not responsible for changing demand, but those in growing markets will earn higher wages than those in declining markets. This might be considered inequitable because the workers have done nothing to deserve such differences. The more difficult is mobility and the less elastic the flow supply curve, the more wages can diverge upward or downward from their equilibrium levels and the longer such divergences can persist. Equity could be imposed on such a structure of submarkets in two ways: wage rates other than the market rates could be imposed, or post-tax incomes of workers could be modified by taxes and transfers without affecting pre-tax wage rates.

The former technique would necessarily cause a shortage of labour in any submarket in which the wage rate is reduced and a surplus of labour, or unemployment, in any submarket in which the wage rate is increased. Taxes and transfers would not have this effect, however, except with respect to the willingness to work. Employers would still have to pay the pre-tax market wage, but any worker who withdrew from the labour market would sacrifice only the post-tax wage. If the imposition of an income tax resulted in more workers choosing not to work because of the fall in the post-tax wage rate, the pre-tax wage would increase. If the payment of transfers were geared to income rather than employment, the net wage from employment would fall, and if this led to some withdrawal of labour, pre-tax wage rates would again increase.

Since the equilibrium without taxes and transfers is perfectly efficient, any tax and transfer scheme that leads to withdrawal of some workers will cause inefficiency. But for any target distribution of post-tax income, a tax system that causes distortion only to the extent that it leads to voluntary withdrawal from employment would have less serious consequences for efficiency than would the imposition of nonmarket pre-tax wages, for the latter would cause distorting incentives for employers as well as employees. In low wage submarkets, a transfer payment not dependent on employment might encourage some workers to withdraw, while an imposed wage above the equilibrium might encourage more to seek employment. They would not secure employment, however, because the higher pre-tax wage would cause a reduced demand for labour.

Any narrowing of post-tax wage differentials from their free market levels will reduce the net flow of workers among submarkets, and it is that flow that reduces the differentials that cause the inequity. In figure 1(b) the level of the flow supply curve is determined by wage rates in other submarkets, and the net flow is then determined by the wage rate in the submarket in question. When wages rise elsewhere and fall in the submarket in question, the flow supply curve shifts upward while the wage falls, causing a net outflow of workers. If the perceived inequity is corrected by policy that transfers income from the workers in submarkets with increased wages to those in submarkets with reduced wages, the taxes will cause the flow supply curve to fall and the subsidies will cause the wage rate to rise. Both forces reduce the net outflow.

Thus policies that achieve equity by narrowing disequilibrium post-tax wage differentials will impede the achievement of efficiency in both the static and dynamic workings of the market. Imposed pre-tax wages, as we have seen, result in labour shortages and inefficient use of scarce labour in submarkets where wages are reduced by policy and unemployment in submarkets where imposed wages are above the market level.

Tax and transfer schemes typically fail to distinguish between wage differentials that result from long-run equilibrium and those that result from long-run disequilibrium. Shifts in demand cause changes in short-run equilibrium wages and induce net flows of labour that in time restore long-run equilibrium. During the adjustment period there is inequity. But there are also long-run equilibrium wage differentials that reflect differences in skill levels and the costs of acquiring human capital. If these are reduced, the incentive to acquire skill is reduced and there is inefficiently low investment in human capital. Narrowing of wage differentials by policies that fail to distinguish long-run disequilibrium from long-run equilibrium differentials may achieve equity in the former case, albeit at the expense of efficiency in the use of labour, but cause vertical inequity in the latter case by reducing differentials that equitably reflect differences in the costs of acquiring human capital.

The free market is self-correcting, but the process of correction by labour mobility may be slow and inequities are generated during the adjustment process. While the narrowing of differentials corrects the inequity of long-run disequilibrium, it reduces the incentive for the dynamic correction process. Thus the cause of inequity persists and the need for policy persists longer than would be the case without such policies. Anything that impedes labour mobility impedes the efficient process of adjustment to changes in the relative demands for labour in different submarkets. It is for this reason that policies that reduce the incentive for mobility are often accompanied by policies of subsidized retraining and relocation that increase such incentives. Transfers and subsidies both cost money. Even if they are offsetting in their effects on efficient mobility, their combined cost must be met by taxes that inevitably impede efficiency wherever they are imposed.

In the spot market the individual worker is the self-proprietor of human capital to the maximum possible extent. Tomorrow's wage rate depends on market forces over which he has no control. Integrity is satisfied only because there are no promises to break. The worker bears the risk inherent in changing market forces, but so does the employer. If the wage rate rises in a submarket, the worker is better off but the employer is worse off. If the wage rate falls, the worker is worse off and the employer better off. Both parties may agree to hedge the risk in the futures market. This may be done by agreeing today on a contract of work for tomorrow for a wage specified in advance. When the contract is agreed for a defined period into the future, we have the defined period contract.

So far we have assumed that information, search, training, and negotiation costs are zero. In the real world, of course, these can be substantial and arise every time a contract is made. It is accordingly more efficient in cases where the job is continuous for labour to be hired for a week rather than a day, and for a month rather than a week. This is the second reason why defined period contracts may be preferred to the spot labour market.

THE DEFINED PERIOD CONTRACT

If all period contracts were for the same period of time, and all expired simultaneously, the period market would have the same characteristics as the spot market. The same forces of changing demand that gave rise to changing wage differentials among submarkets on a daily basis would now cause changes only monthly or annually. Those changes would be more marked the longer the time period of the contract, and would be intensified by speculative anticipation of continuing trends. The corrective mechanism of mobility would not begin to operate until the contract renewal date. While such a market might economize in negotiation costs, it would be less flexible than the spot market and less efficient in the process of dynamic adjustment. Large changes in wage differentials that had been pent up during the contract period would be more inequitable than small changes on a day to day basis.

When contracts of different length coexist, however, and contracts of the same length do not have simultaneous expiry dates, the defined period market can be both more efficient and more equitable than the spot market. A worker entering the labour force, or an existing worker with a contract about to expire, would decide whether to enter the spot market or to accept a contract for a short or long defined period. Employers would have the same options. Longer periods would be more efficient where mobility costs are high and would be more appealing to persons with high risk aversity. The advantage of longer contracts would depend on their enforceability and the principle of integrity would be important. In a free and flexible labour market of this type the equilibrium wage rates for contracts of different lengths may well differ, just as spot and future prices in commodity markets differ. The wage rates for new contracts in different submarkets would adjust to changing demand, but the wage rate would not change during the life of a contract except as specified in the contract.

At any time, two workers performing the same type of work for the same employer could receive different wage rates if they had contracts of different lengths or with different expiry dates. This might appear to violate the principle of horizontal equity, but it is questionable whether equity is violated when workers choose contracts of different lengths, knowing that they involve different wage rates. The future course of wages and prices is always uncertain. Inevitably some persons will choose contract periods that they will subsequently regret, just as decisions about mortgage periods, the buying of short-term or long-term bonds, insurance contracts, and gambling are often regretted in the light of hindsight. In a labour market in which contracts of different lengths are freely available, at wage rates determined by market forces, it is questionable whether equity is violated when all employers and employees face the same options. Given the real existence of mobility costs, the worker must speculate about the future when he chooses his occupation. Some acquire specialized skills and subsequently regret their choices when the future course of relative wages becomes known. The long period contract permits the individual to hedge the uncertainty associated with the choice of occupation. Equity cannot be violated by a free choice to hedge an existing uncertainty.

The defined period contract contains implicit limits to the extent to which the wage rate can in future differ from the wage rate then prevailing in the spot market or for new contracts. In a submarket in which the demand for labour increases unexpectedly, the wage rate will increase. New recruits may receive higher wages than those who entered long period contracts some time ago. But a long period contract can always be broken on payment of liquidated damages. If those damages are low, workers will terminate long period contracts and enter new ones. The higher the liquidated damages, the greater the difference in wages must be before default becomes worth-while. In a submarket in which the demand for labour falls the wage rate will fall. Workers with long period contracts will receive higher wages than those on new contracts. The employer now has the incentive to terminate the existing long period contracts, and this he can do on payment of damages.

The value of a defined period contract depends on its enforceability. The degree of security is specified by the extent of liquidated damages for default. If the specified wage rates for short and long period contracts are equal, we should expect the liquidated damages for default by the two parties to be of comparable magnitude. They can be low for either party, or high for either party. Low damages indicate an implicit agreement that the contract may be terminated if wages rates in future differ slightly from those specified in the contract. High damages imply agreement that the contract will remain binding even though significant differences from current wages subsequently emerge. The subsequent appearance of horizontal inequity then results from the free decision of the parties to a long period contract to specify high liquidated damages for default.

Liquidated damages for default need not be equal for the two parties. Typically they will be greater for the employer, who may be bound to pay the full specified wage for the life of the contract, while the employee cannot be bound by indenture and can at most lose pension rights, seniority pay, or terminal bonus. If the employer is more committed to the contract than the employee, then there will be consideration for that asymmetry in the wage rate, which would be lower for a long period contract than for a short period. The employee who chooses the long period is then essentially buying job insurance from the employer. His wage rate would be lower than that of a fellow worker on a short period contract, but this clearly would not constitute horizontal inequity when he has chosen to pay for security.

Defined period contracts expire at the end of the period. Wage rates in different submarkets will adjust to changing demand just as they do in spot markets, and workers in submarkets with high wages will be able to enter more favourable new contracts than workers in submarkets with low wages. In principle the defined period contract is subject to the same inequities as the spot market. But inequitable differentials could emerge only with mobility costs. With perfect mobility such differentials could not arise and persist in either spot or defined period markets. The defined period market differs from the spot market in the incidence of inequity and the dynamics of mobility.

In the spot market a change in demand is reflected instantly in a changed wage rate for all workers in the submarket. It takes time to move to a different submarket and during the time lag there are inequitable wage differentials. With defined period contracts, however, a change in demand has no effect on the wage rate during the contract period. The impact of changing demand is focused on new contracts. The demand for labour by any employer relates the total number of workers employed to the wage rate. If workers are hired for twelve month contracts, only one-twelfth of their contracts fall due for renewal each month. A 5 per cent reduction in the demand for labour during one month is a 60 per cent reduction in the number of new contracts written that month. The effect of this leverage is that while wage rates remain unchanged for workers during their contracts, the spot wage and the wage rate for new contracts will change much more than they would if there were no defined period contracts. If the employer believes the reduction in demand for labour to be temporary, then he will severely curtail hiring in the spot market, but continue to commit workers to defined period contracts. The spot wage rate will fall more than the wage for defined periods. If the decline in demand is perceived as a trend, however, the employer will prefer not to commit himself to new long period contracts and the wage rate for defined terms may fall more than the spot rate.[1]

Thus the immediate incidence of wage changes is selective. Fluctuations in demand for labour will be focused on the spot wage. To the extent that the consequence is inequitable, the inequity is suffered by those workers who chose to bear the risk. Those who protected themselves from uncertainty by entering longer period contracts are protected. Trends in demand, however, are clearly signalled by greater reductions in the wage rate for new period contracts. Those whose period contracts are about to expire may either choose to remain in the submarket with new defined period contracts at lower wages, or seek refuge in the spot market while they arrange to move to a different submarket. Workers whose defined term contracts do not expire for some time are given clear notice of the trend and can plan in advance the move to a different submarket that will be appropriate when their contracts expire.

If the expiry date of a defined period contract is rigid, both parties may experience a marked change in the wage rate when a new contract is entered into. Both parties will have received market signals of wage trends and may have made the necessary plans for alternatives to contract renewal. The parties can always change the termination date of an existing contract by agreement, however. If two years of a three year contract have elapsed, for example, the parties may agree to replace the existing contract with a new three year contract. If the wage trend in the submarket is downward, the new contract may be for a lower wage rate. The employee has then voluntarily suffered a fall in the wage rate, although his old contract was valid for a further year, in exchange for an additional two year promise of employment, during which he can plan to move to another submarket. If the wage trend is upward, the employer would have suffered an immediate wage increase in order to secure the services of the worker for a further two years. The willingness or unwillingness of the parties to extend contracts in this way will itself give clear signals of what to expect when the current contract expires.

The flexible use of defined period contracts, and the variety of lengths, conditions, and provision for default they can encompass, makes it possible to avoid much of the inequity of the spot market. Uncertainty can be hedged and mobility planned on the basis of advance notice from clear market signals. The apparent horizontal inequity of wage differentials that emerge from changing demand is focused precisely on those who choose to remain in the spot market. It is questionable whether there is any inequity when some gain and some lose unexpectedly as the result of risks that both choose to bear. But the defined period contract provides an escape from inequity only if the terms of the contract are specified and enforced. The system depends on the principle of integrity. If the agreed terms of such contracts are overridden by unexpected policy changes, such policies violate integrity and may be a cause in inequity. If, for example, one worker chooses a long period contract at a low wage, and another chooses a short period contract at high wage, then the wage difference is the equitable price of job security. If subsequent changes in law grant the worker with the short period contract the same degree of job security as that enjoyed by the worker with the long period contract, then the wage difference becomes inequitable. The same inequity arises if the job security of the long period contract is violated in ways not provided for by liquidated damages.

The practice of extending the term of a contract may become habitual. For example, new terms may be negotiated for the next three years every time the contract has only one year to expiry. Such a contract may alternatively be viewed as a contract for an indefinite term, subject to one year's notice by either party of an intention to permit is to expire. The difference between these cases lies in the residual expectation. The defined period contract is expected to expire unless it is explicitly extended or renewed. The indefinite term contract is expected to continue unless it is explicitly terminated. When expiry is expected, there will be no liquidated damages for non-renewal. But when continuation is expected, there may be either explicit or implicit damages for termination.

THE INDEFINITE PERIOD CONTRACT

The simplest form of the indefinite period contract is an extension of the spot market. In that market the worker is hired for the day and market forces determine the wage rate. With costless mobility, expanding firms can find new workers and workers released from contracting firms can find new jobs, the total number of jobs being adjusted to the number of workers by the flexible competitive wage. While the movement of workers is the mechanism that maintains equilibrium, most workers serve the same employers on consecutive days. In the spot market the contract expires at the end of the day and has to be explicitly renewed for the next day. Since the majority of contracts are renewed, the simpler arrangement is the agreed presumption that the contract is renewed, at the market wage for the next day, unless either party decides to terminate it. This is an indefinite period contract. If the wage is determined daily by market forces beyond the control of either party and there are no provisions for liquidated damages on termination, there is no difference of substance between the spot and indefinite period contracts.

In practice even a competitive market does not clear instantly and perfectly, and there are costs of search and mobility. A
worker advised one evening that he will not be employed the
next day may be unable to find a new job immediately. He
may be unemployed for a day or two and incur relocation
costs. The employer who is advised one evening that the worker
will not be available the next day may be unable to find another worker instantly and may incur search costs. Both parties may then agree that termination of the indefinite period
contract requires some period of notice, or alternatively, some
monetary compensation. Liquidated damages for termination are
then part of the contract. Such a contractual arrangement fully
satisfies the criteria of efficiency, equity, and integrity. It is
more efficient than the spot market, for the costs of search
and mobility are incurred only when necessary rather than by
each party every day. But integrity is satisfied only when the
wage at which the contract continues is specified. If a perfect
market clearly signals an equilibrium wage, it may be agreed
that the wage will be the equilibrium wage on a day to day
basis.

In practice even a competitive market does not instantly
achieve a single wage rate for all workers. An expanding firm
may have to offer a wage premium to attract new workers and
workers released from a contracting firm may offer their services at below the existing wage to encourage another firm to
employ them. It is precisely the existence of wage offers above
or below the existing wage that causes the equilibrium to adjust. When the cost of mobility is very low, such discrepancies will be small. But they still leave the precise level of the
equilibrium wage ambiguous, and the wage for indefinite term
contracts is not precisely specified. If search and mobility costs
are significant, the discrepancies in wage rates might be significant.

It is the existence of search and mobility costs that gives
rise to the central problem of the indefinite term contract.
While liquidated damages can protect each party from the costs
caused by failure of the other party to continue with the contract, no automatic mechanism specifies without ambiguity
what the wage rate of the continuing contract should be. Even
if full data on all other contracts were freely available, the
employee and the employer could interpret them to yield different estimates of the equilibrium wage. While repetitive search
costs are avoided by the indefinite term contract, the costs of
daily negotiation of the wage rate are not. If the parties fail

to agree on the wage, it is not clear which has terminated the continuing contract, and which should pay the liquidated damages.

The continuous ambiguity concerning the level of the equilibrium wage means that it cannot be used as an automatic system to determine the wage rate of an indefinite period contract. The wage rate must be specified by agreement between the parties. The costs of negotiation and uncertainty are reduced when the wage rate is specified for a defined period into the future. That is the rationale of the defined period contract. But if the parties agree to an indefinite period contract, with liquidated damages for termination by either party, but agree on the wage rate for only a defined period, then when that period expires there is commitment to continuation of an unspecified contract. Each party may agree to continuation on his own terms but not the other's, each may claim default by the other, and the meaning and purpose of the liquidated damages break down. The principle of integrity requires that promises be honoured, but a system in which each party is bound by promises that are not clearly specified is not viable. If the contract is to be for an indefinite period, then the wage rate should be specified for an indefinite period. There are, however, serious difficulties involved in specifying a wage rate into the indefinite future.

The obvious way to specify a wage rate is in money terms. Many indefinite period contracts specify little more than the nature of the job, the money wage rate, and the required notice of termination. With rising prices, a specified money wage is a falling real wage. If the employee suffers no loss of deferred compensation by terminating the contract, and his search and mobility costs are negligible, a fall in the real wage will motivate employees to move to better contracts with other employers. To prevent this, employers will agree to increase the money wage rate to maintain it at an equilibrium level for new contracts.

If mobility costs are significant for the employee, however, the real wage can be allowed to fall significantly before employees will be persuaded to move. In order to retain workers, it is only necessary for the employer to maintain the real wage at the competitive level less the maximum differential that employees will accept rather than terminate the contract. The employee's mobility cost may well increase with time. Relocation of a family is more expensive than relocation of a single person. With family responsibilities the individual becomes more risk averse and the uncertainty costs of the search process increase. After some years of service, the employee may enjoy a higher wage rate or other benefits of seniority and accumulated rights in a pension plan that would be sacrificed on termination. If the costs for the worker of terminating employment rise with the passage of time, and if wages are specified in money terms, it becomes possible for employers to permit real wages to fall through inflation to a greater extent for senior than junior employees. New recruits, however, must be paid the current equilibrium wage. The effect of inflation is that seniority differentials are reduced and new workers may even be paid more than workers with some years of service. Clearly this violates the principle of vertical equity.

Mobility costs arise for employers as well as for employees, however. The senior employee would suffer loss of seniority if he moved to a different employer because his specialized knowledge and experience of the firm would be less valuable elsewhere. But the employer depends on that specialized knowledge and may experience considerable difficulty and cost in finding as valuable a replacement worker. Both become dependent on continuing employment. If the employer has the power to set the wage rate, he can exploit the rent from specialized knowledge by depressing the real wage of a senior worker with confidence that the worker will be reluctant to move. But if the worker specifies the wage rate, he can exploit the rent by raising his demands in the confident expectation that the employer cannot afford to lose him. When the wage is negotiated there may be a wide range of indeterminacy between the minimum the worker would accept rather then move and the maximum the employer would pay rather than lose him. Inflation itself tends to work to the advantage of the employer, because the employee must continuously push the money wage up simply to maintain a constant real wage. The time lag that usually occurs between a rise in the cost of living and an offsetting adjustment in the money wage rate favours the employer. But the boom conditions that often accompany inflation work to the advantage of the employee. When there is full employment and businesses are expanding, the employee would find alternative employment more readily available, while the employer would have greater difficulty in finding an alternative employee.

The consequences of inflation are easily avoided by specifying the wage rate in real terms. The simplest such specification is agreement on an initial money wage with provision for periodic adjustment by the change in the consumer price index. Such COLA clauses have become quite common in indefinite period contracts. But the equilibrium real wage for a particular employee will change over time for many reasons that are not easy to specify in advance. Growth in per capita income in the economy as a whole leads to rising equilibrium real wages. Changes in the composition of demand causes increases in the equilibrium real wage in some submarkets and decreases in others. It is largely because of the anticipated possibility that some real wage rates may fall that COLA clauses are neither universal nor guaranteed indefinitely. The progress of the individual employee to higher paid positions of greater responsibility is impossible to forecast at the beginning of his employment. Yet his expectations of promotion are part of the criterion of remuneration that persuades him to commit himself to the indefinite period contract.

It is in principle possible to specify the terms and conditions of the indefinite period contract with many clauses and contingency provisions. The money wage can be tied to economic indices of prices and national income, changing market conditions can be reflected in profit-sharing schemes, promotion can be tied to years of service or the decision to promote delegated to promotion committees. The more complicated the contract, the greater are the costs of negotiating it. Because it is impossible to specify every contingency in advance, the precise response to changing economic conditions is not specified explicitly. Instead there is the common understanding, or implicit contract, that wage rates will be adjusted "fairly" to changing conditions.[2] The costs of negotiation would be prohibitive if the employer had to negotiate separately with each new recruit. The common practice, therefore, is for the employer to specify the standard terms of the contract which the potential recruit is free either to accept or reject.

The indefinite period contract inevitably contains the paradox that both parties are committed to it on a continuing basis while the precise terms of the contract to which they are committed are not specified. The unavoidable costs of search, relocation, and retraining mean that each party suffers if the other terminates the contract. Those costs may be matched by liquidated damages for default. But this raises the further ambiguity as to who has defaulted when the continuing terms of the contract are not agreed. Advance specification of the way in which the money wage should adjust to various forces gives rise to negotiation costs and it is impossible to foresee all contingencies. It would not be rational to achieve further refinement of advance specification when the cost of doing so exceeds the potential costs of not doing so. The latter costs are limited to the costs incurred by termination of the contract if there is subsequent failure to agree. In practice the employer specifies the terms of the offer of employment, and the employer retains flexibility if these are left vague. With a long-term trend for money wages to rise, the less that increases are promised in advance, the less committed is the employer.

When the conditions of the contract are specified in advance, the principle of integrity requires that they be honoured. If they are honoured in terms that both parties initially agreed, there is no problem of inequity. When the conditions become obsolete, the parties may agree to revise them. If they agree, there is again no problem of equity. But failure to agree leaves the paradox of commitment to an unspecified contract, and the resolution of that paradox can only be by appeal to the criterion of equity.

I have so far discussed the contract of employment as a voluntary arrangement between two individuals, the employer and the employee. There are strong reasons on grounds of efficiency for using defined period or indefinite period contracts rather than spot contracts, but period contracts require periodic renegotiation of their terms. The high costs of separate negotiation with each employee have been overcome by the practice of collective bargaining. The agencies of collective negotiation can take many forms, of which the formal trade union is only one. I shall use the term "union" in a generic sense to describe all such employees' agencies to collective negotiation, for I am concerned with the process rather than the legal status, rights, and responsibilities that distinguish the "trade union" in its specific sense from other such agencies. It is to the role of the union in the labour market that we now turn our attention.

CHAPTER FOUR

Collective Bargaining

The contract of employment between employer and employee, each acting as a single individual, is the basic unit of the labour market. Each party to a contract is in principle free to negotiate its terms with the other party. Individual negotiation is in fact the way in which the terms of employment are determined for unique employees. The small firm that hires only a few workers, no two of whom have comparable qualifications and perform identical tasks, must determine the wage separately for each. In the large firm, senior employees may have jobs or qualifications different from those of other employees and again the wage is settled by individual bargaining. But individual negotiation is not the common practice when the firm employs many workers who are comparably qualified and perform identical tasks.

In theory a competitive market works because large numbers of individuals separately negotiate contracts. Each buyer can buy from any of several sellers and each seller can sell to any of several buyers. The continuous making and revising of offers is the process that establishes an equilibrium price towards which all individual contracts converge. But when one seller sells identical goods to many different buyers, the cost of negotiating a price separately with each becomes prohibitive. The practice of haggling does prevail in the real estate and car markets, for example, where negotiation costs are low in relation to the value of the transaction, and in bazaars, where a low value is placed on time spent haggling. The common practice in goods markets, however, is for the seller to set a price that each buyer is free to accept or reject. If too many buyers accept, the seller raises the price, and if too many reject, he reduces it. Such feedback enables the market to work in determining an equilibrium price without the need for individual bargaining. One feature of such a process is that all buyers at a particular time pay the same price for identical items.

A similar process operates in the labour market, but in this case the buyer, or employer, buys from many individual sellers, or employees. The common practice is therefore for the employer to state the wage rate that the potential employee is free to accept or reject. If too many are willing to accept, the wage rate may be revised downward, and if too many reject, it may be increased. Such a market can work to determine an equilibrium wage if there are several competing employers, and workers are free to accept the best offer and to change employers whenever a better opportunity is available. The spot labour market works in this way. Such a process economizes in negotiation costs and workers who perform the same task for the same employer receive equal wage rates.

The problem with a labour market in which the employer states the wage rate is that in practice employees do not have complete flexibility to transfer to other competing employers. When search and mobility costs are significant, the employee would rather continue to work for his present employer than move to a different job even if another employer offers a higher wage rate. The greater the search and mobility costs, the greater can the wage differential be without being sufficient to persuade workers to move. Employers may compete effectively for new entrants to the labour market, but need not pay market equilibrium wages in order to retain their current workers.

The cost a worker incurs if he decides to change his job rises with age and years of service. The monetary and personal costs of relocation rise with the growth of family responsibilities and the ties of family members to the current location. The sacrifice of seniority, pension rights, and the value of accumulated experience of the current employer's operations increase with years of service. The cost of changing employment is independent of the length of time that the new employment is expected to last. A young worker with a whole career ahead of him may consider the cost of relocating to be worth-while, while an older worker with fewer years remaining before retirement may not. For all these reasons mobility costs tie senior workers more strongly to their current employers than they do junior workers. This makes it possible for employers to exploit senior workers more than junior employees.

In theory the immobility of workers should permit employers to reduce the wage rate once workers have become sufficiently committed to the employer to be unwilling to incur the costs of moving to a different job. With rising prices, real wage rates can be allowed to fall even though money wage rates are increased, provided that they are increased by less than the inflation rate. In practice, employers may be reluctant to exercise their power to exploit immobile workers. Firms acquire reputations among workers just as they do among customers. A firm that is well regarded as a fair employer may find it easier to recruit good new workers than one that acquires a reputation for unscrupulous exploitation. The desire to maintain goodwill with both existing and potential workers may limit the extent to which the power to depress wages is exercised in practice. The extent of the employer's power in theory will depend on whether the employer is able to set wages separately for existing workers and for new workers.

Rising product prices increase the profit of the firm. At current wage rates more workers are worth hiring. The demand for labour increases and, with a given supply of labour, the effect of competition is to increase the wage rate. In this way a perfectly competitive labour market maintains real wage rates despite inflation. When existing workers are immobile, however, competition does not necessarily operate to force employers to increase wages. Competition works when different employers compete on equal terms for the same employees. With immobility, however, each firm has an automatic advantage over its rivals in dealing with its own employees. With rising prices it becomes profitable to employ more workers and there is an excess demand for labour. But each employer is reluctant to compete for additional workers by offering a higher wage rate if he would have to increase the wage equally for his existing workers. If, for example, it would be necessary to increase the wage rate by 5 per cent to attract enough new workers to increase the firm's labour force by 5 per cent, the total wage bill would increase by over 10 per cent. The extra cost of hiring additional workers would effectively be twice their wage rate. While additional workers would be worth hiring at the current wage, they may not be worth hiring at twice the current wage. Instead, firms compete for additional workers in ways other than by offering higher wages. With a given supply of labour, all firms can maintain their labour force and there are enough new recruits to fill vacancies arising from death or retirement. There is a shortage of labour, for each firm would like to expand, but the wage rate does not increase if no firm is willing to meet the cost of increasing wages for its current workers in order to attract additional ones. There is no need for collusion among firms to keep wages down, but the wage rate remains below the competitive level.

The second possibility arises if the firm is able to offer a higher wage rate for new recruits without increasing the wage rate for existing workers. It then becomes possible for firms to compete for new workers by offering higher wages, without incurring the cost of increased wages for existing workers. Competition among employers would then establish an equilibrium wage for new entrants to the labour force, while established workers would be paid less than their competitive equilibrium wage because mobility costs prevent competition from operating for established workers. It may in practice be very difficult to offer new workers a wage higher than that for existing workers. But if experienced workers are normally paid more than new recruits, it may be simple to raise the wage for new recruits and thereby reduce the seniority differential. Experienced workers would be paid more than new recruits, but not as much more as would result from competitive forces, because experienced workers are sufficiently tied to their current employers to be unable to take advantage of effective competition through mobility. While a reduction in seniority differentials would inflict inequity on the current generation of senior employees, the firm would gain no continuing advantage. New entrants to the labour market are attracted by future prospects as well as by the starting wage. Once they learn that seniority differentials are smaller, their own future prospects appear less attractive and they will accept employment only at a higher initial wage. If new workers know the current seniority differentials and base their own expectations on them, there is no reason why the equilibrium current value of lifetime earnings in the occupation should change. The employer, however, will have lost the security that high seniority differentials previously provided in their role as a deterrent to mobility. Unless the employer perceives some advantage to him of reducing the liquidated damages for withdrawal from the contract by the employee, he will be reluctant to reduce seniority differentials permanently and may be deterred from exploiting his power to take advantage of his current senior workers. If the power to raise the wage rate for new workers but not for existing senior workers is not used, this case has results no different from the previous case in which that power was absent.

How far would a labour market, in which employers exercise these powers, satisfy the criteria of efficiency, equity, and integrity? The criterion of efficiency is met to a very high degree. The excess demand for labour means that labour will be fully utilized. This is the essence of the mechanism by which, in Keynesian theory, inflation achieves full employment. The allocation of existing labour is constrained by the costs of mobility and there is competition for new entrants to the labour force. If there is a shortage of labour but wages for new recruits do not increase, then they are not necessarily allocated to the employment where their services are most highly valued. Efficient allocation could still occur, however, if nonwage competition for new recruits reflects the values placed on them by competing employers. For the worker, the wage rate is the price of leisure. If wage rates remain below the competitive level, the price of leisure is too low, and some potential workers who could be employed profitably may withdraw from the labour force. It is questionable, however, whether this effect would be very significant. If there is wage discrimination between junior and senior workers so that the wage for new recruits is at the competitive level, then the criterion of efficiency is fully met. A system in which the employer states the wage, while the worker can only accept or reject the offer, clearly minimizes the costs of bargaining. The employer incurs the costs of acquiring the information about the labour market on which his offer is based, while the employee incurs the cost of assessing whether to accept it. There is no reason to suppose that these costs will be greater than they would be in a context of bargaining, however, while the cost of bargaining itself is avoided.

The principle of equity is not fully satisfied, however. If new recruits are paid more than existing workers, there is horizontal inequity and if seniority differentials are reduced, there is vertical inequity. The major inequity, however, concerns the distribution of rents between employees and employers. With high search and mobility costs, the employer would be willing to pay a wage above the perfectly competitive level rather than lose the worker, while the worker would accept a wage below the competitive level rather than move. The difference between the most that the employer would pay and the least that the employee would accept represents the margin of rent that must somehow be divided between them. In a perfectly competitive market with no mobility costs that margin is zero. But with mobility costs the margin can be significant and when the employer sets the wage rate he naturally chooses the minimum the employee is expected to accept. The employer then receives the entire margin of rent. It is in this sense that the employer "exploits" the worker, for the wage falls short of the value of the worker's contribution to output by the costs that mobility would impose on the worker. Such mobility costs provide the employer with a captive labour force and the employer can take advantage of his protection from effective competition by paying lower wages. The current employer can retain his workers at a lower wage than any competitor would have to offer to entice them to move. A new firm attempting to enter the industry would have to pay higher wage rates than existing firms to attract senior and experienced workers. Unless a new firm could function entirely with inexperienced new entrants to the labour force, the mobility costs of senior workers will constitute a barrier to entry. If only the existing firms compete for new entrants, the starting wage will be below the competitive level since no firm will be willing to increase wage rates for all its workers in order to attract additional new recruits. Thus the effect of a labour market in which mobility costs are high and the employer sets the wage rate is that profits, or the returns to capital, are higher and wages are lower than would be the case with zero mobility costs and perfect competition. It is, of course, precisely the high rate of return to capital that makes the employment of labour profitable and results in full employment or, in the absence of discrimination, in a shortage of labour.

Whether the principle of integrity is violated will depend upon whether any promises are broken. Explicit contractual commitments are not likely to be violated, but the reasonable expectations of the employee and implicit promises by the employer may well be. The worker who is persuaded to join a firm by the promise of increasing wages with seniority, for example, who subsequently finds that his real wage is eroded by inflation, while increased wages for new recruits reduce the seniority differential, may well feel justifiably aggrieved.[1] The extent of such "exploitation" is of course directly related to the level of mobility costs that deter the senior worker from moving to a different job. This problem was discussed in chapter 2. The worker has become tied to a continuing contract with his present employer without enforceable statement of the terms of the contract to which he is committed. The captive status of the worker is the prerequisite for exploitation.

The converse of a market in which the employer sets the wage is one in which the employee states the wage at which he is willing to work, leaving the potential employer free to accept or reject the offer. This is the common case with professional practitioners when one worker serves several clients. The casual or intermittent nature of the employment contract makes this a spot market. Each buyer of services typically employs only one professional worker, and then only as the need arises, while the worker serves several clients or employers. The worker sells a service to many customers and typically states his price. In continuing contracts of employment, however, the worker serves only one employer who may employ several workers. If each worker separately states the wage at which he is willing to work and the workers are comparably qualified, the employer will naturally hire those willing to work for the lowest wages. In effect the employer sets the cut-off wage below which he accepts offers to work and above which he does not. There is then no difference in principle whether the offer is made by the employer or the employee. A competitive market works either way if the workers are interchangeable.

Once a worker is employed, however, his replacement by a different worker would give rise to costs of search and training for the employer as well as mobility costs for the employee. Each party becomes committed to the other and in principle either party could take advantage of the other's commitment. The employer could state a wage below the competitive level, which the worker would rather accept than move, and the employee could state a wage above the competitive level which the employer would rather pay than incur the costs of replacing him. The asymmetry arises from the fact that there are typically several employees in the firm but only one employer. If each employee states his wage separately, the employer must determine his cut-off level. Workers stating the highest wages may find their offers rejected and regret that they did not ask for less, for they would have been willing to accept less rather then move. Workers asking for low wages may find that their colleagues' higher offers are accepted, and regret that they did not ask for more. The costs to the employer of replacing a few workers may be small, while the disruption to the operation of the firm caused by the need to replace many would be severe. Clearly it is to the advantage of the workers to collude.

If all set the same wage for their services, the employer must either accept or reject it. He may choose to reject some offers in order to reduce the size of his workforce, but he has no incentive to replace a few workers and would find it very costly to replace them all. Thus the workers tend to state a single wage for the job in question if they set the wage, just as the employer states a single wage if he sets it. The process of collusion among the workers requires some organization, and that organization is a union. The union can take many forms, from a loose association to a rigidly structured body. The important feature is that the union can speak for all workers with a single voice and thus has as much power to set the wage at which they will continue to work as the employer has power to set the wage at which he will continue to employ them.

WAGE DETERMINATION
WITH UNIONS

The union provides both knowledge and power for the workers. In a perfectly competitive labour market all parties have ready access to knowledge of the various offers available. In the real world, however, the worker does not have ready access to all relevant information. In order to determine the minimum wage for which he would be willing to continue in his present employment, the worker must know the alternatives. Assembling current information about the wage rates in other firms, other locations, and other occupations, together with an assessment of the probability of finding other employment, needs both time and skill. The individual may have very little idea what his alternative opportunities are, and neither know nor appreciate how high the search costs might be in finding other work, nor how great the mobility costs would be in lost seniority and pension rights if he left his current employment. Cautious individuals may underestimate their prospects elsewhere, overestimate search and mobility costs, and set the minimum wage they should accept in their current jobs too low. Others may err in the opposite direction, set their reservation wage too high and learn the costs of changing jobs only by painful experience. The union can assemble the relevant information at a small cost per worker when the number of members in the union is large. While it was not the original purpose of unions, the research function of unions is today a very important part of their role.

Assessment of the maximum wage the employer would be willing to pay rather than lose his workers is more difficult, yet that figure is the target wage for employees who wish to maximize their share of the rents that derive from mobility costs. The ability of the employer to pay higher wages from current profits, to reflect higher wages in higher prices, to recruit and train other workers, or to withstand a work stoppage cannot be estimated without knowledge of the employer's current circumstances and appropriate interpretation of that knowledge. To predict the reaction of management to wage demands by workers calls for the ability to think like management. Both assembly of the relevant information and its appropriate interpretation are tasks more readily achieved by a well-organized union than the individual worker.

Knowledge is the source of power. The employer who sets a wage rate that individual employees can only accept or reject can use that power to maximum advantage only if the alternative options open to employees can be assessed. A large firm with a good personnel office has the relevant knowledge. If workers are to state the wage to maximum advantage, they must similarly understand the employer's position. A well-organized union with a good research staff can provide that understanding. Thus a good union can wield, on behalf of its members, power in the process of wage setting comparable with that wielded by the employer. If both have all relevant information and are able to assess it appropriately, then both have the necessary source of power. But if both have power, neither has total power over the other. If both have the power to state the wage rate, then neither confronts a party that can only accept or reject. Offer is met by counter offer and a process of bargaining ensues. If both parties know the maximum wage that the employer would pay and the minimum that the workers would accept, then both know the potential range for bargaining. But knowledge of that range does not suffice to determine the outcome within that range.

While in practice neither party can predict the other's reaction with accuracy or absolute confidence, we can simplify the

essence of the bargaining situation by assuming that each knows
the reservation wage of the other. The union knows the maximum that the employer would pay rather than lose his labour
force, and the employer knows the minimum that the workers
would accept rather than find alternative employment. If the
two reservation wage rates are equal, as they would be in a
perfectly competitive market, the outcome of the bargaining
process would be determined and immediately achieved, for
both offers would be identical. If the employer's reservation
wage exceeds the workers', then any wage rate between them
would constitute a *pareto optimal* contract for both. Both parties would be better off than if there were no contract. What
wage rate eventually prevails will depend upon the balance of
bargaining power, but the balance of power is far from the
simple idea that superficial consideration of the matter would
suggest.[2]

The simplest models of the bargaining process perceive it as
a balance of static forces. Analysis by the techniques of comparative statics suffices when power is either absent or concentrated. In a model of perfect competition, neither party has
the power to impose a wage other than the competitive equilibrium. That equilibrium can be determined by analysis of static
forces. If the equilibrium has stability properties, there is no
need to consider the complexities of the dynamic process of
adjustment by which equilibrium is achieved. The outcome is
the same whatever the path of adjustment to equilibrium, and
the adjustment is presumed to be instantaneous. The same is
true when only one party has power, whether it be the case
of monopsony, in which the employer states the wage, or monopoly, in which the employees do. The problem is simple when
the potential rent is either zero or accrues entirely to one
party. It is then tempting to assume that when both parties
have some power, the rent will end up divided and the division will depend on the balance of power perceived as the
relative weights of two static forces. The principle of countervailing power[3] suggests that if the parties have comparable
power, the rent will be evenly divided, an outcome that might
be considered both viable and equitable. But such an approach
fails to recognize the essential properties of a bargaining situation.

Negotiation is a form of conflict and conflict is an inherently dynamic process. The outcome of a dynamic adversarial
process depends on the sequence of moves not simply on the

balance of static forces. It is in principle as impossible to predict the outcome of wage negotiations on the basis of an assessment of the relative power of the parties as it is to predict the precise sequence of play in a sporting contest. Each party endeavours to coerce the other to yield. Since yielding involves the sacrifice of the objective sought, a party will yield only if refusal to do so would cause greater sacrifice. The process by which each party threatens to impose penalties on the other to force it to yield is the costly process of bargaining. To be effective threats must be credible, but as most threatened actions would involve costs for both parties, each party knows that the other would be reluctant to follow through on its threats. Bluffs are called and when threats are then kept, both parties do suffer. This process continues until each party has yielded sufficiently for them to reach agreement. Since the process of negotiation is costly for both parties, it is to their common advantage to economize in its use. Once agreement is achieved, the parties commit themselves to it by a binding contract for a defined period, usually from one to three years. The longer the defined period, the more difficult will it be to agree on the terms. A longer contract, however, means a longer period of freedom from the costs of negotiation.[4] The characteristic form of the labour market with collective bargaining is one of an indefinite period contract of employment with the wage rate specified by a series of defined period contracts.

In the discussion of the defined period contract in the previous chapter it was assumed that each worker could negotiate his own contract and different workers performing the same task for the same firm might have contracts of different lengths with different expiry dates. It was argued that such a market would be both efficient and equitable. The range of options open to each party would provide the necessary flexibility for the labour market to adjust smoothly to changing economic forces. With collective bargaining, however, all workers performing the same task in the same firm have defined period contracts of the same length with the same expiry date. The individual no longer has the option to choose his own combination of flexibility and security. While each individual can express his own preferences and the policies of the union may reflect the desires of the majority, the individual worker has no power to determine the outcome of the collective bargaining process. Once the terms of the contract are agreed, the individual can only accept or reject it. He is in essentially the same position as the worker in a market in which the employer states the wage and conditions of employment. In both cases the individual lacks the power to negotiate his own terms and has no freedom of choice among a range of options. The collective bargaining process is less efficient than the market in which the employer sets the wage, by reason of the costs of negotiation and conflict, but the resulting division of the rent between employer and employees may be more equitable.[5] In both cases the principle of horizontal equity is satisfied with respect to the employees of the firm, for all are treated equally.

The major problem with the collective bargaining process is the inefficiency inherent in the process of negotiation and conflict. When different workers negotiate different period contracts at different times, contracts are continuously being made. Changing economic forces impinge on contracts made in the near future, and the prevailing wage rate in a particular occupation adjusts continuously by small changes. The negotiation of each contract is guided by many recent precedents, the range of disagreement is small, and each contract concerns only one worker. Under these conditions the process of bargaining is unlikely to be either prolonged or bitter. With collective bargaining, however, the same contract applies to all workers. When expiry approaches and negotiation begins, it may be some time since the last negotiations. Considerable changes may have taken place in relevant economic conditions that have as yet had no impact on the wage rate in question. These pent up forces are then unleashed at the time of negotiation and the offers of the respective parties will also reflect anticipation of further changes during the life of the contract being negotiated. The two offers may then differ significantly and there is a wide range to be resolved by bargaining. Since the terms of the new contract will apply to all workers for some time to come, small differences in the agreed wage will be of great significance to both sides. When there is a wide difference to resolve and each small step toward resolution means a great deal to both parties, the bargaining is likely to be long and hard.

The contract of employment can have many clauses and several of these may involve disputes in the same negotiations. The process can best be understood, however, if we focus our attention by assuming that there is only one issue, namely the level of the wage rate. We can further assume that each of the parties fully understands the circumstances facing and options open to the other, and that the offers of both parties are realistic in the following sense: the employer would be willing to accept the union's offer if the only alternative were to lose the services of all members of the union; and the employees would be willing to accept the employer's offer if the only alternative were to lose their jobs. Both offers are then within the range of possible contracts, but if search, training, and mobility costs are high, there may be a significant difference between the two offers. If each party believes that the other will, if necessary, accept, then neither will accept. Each will endeavour to persuade the other that it can only accept or reject. Willingness to compromise may be perceived as a sign of weakness and both parties may stubbornly refuse to budge from their entrenched positions.

If both parties know that both offers are within the range of viable contracts, then both know that the outcome will not be rejection in the sense that the employment relationship between the parties will end permanently. They may totally disagree about the wage rate at which employment will continue, but both expect that employment will continue at a wage rate that will eventually be agreed. Thus the option facing each party is not to accept or reject the other's offer but rather to accept the other's offer or to continue with the conflict.[6] Since neither party wishes to yield, both will choose to continue the conflict unless doing so would involve significant costs. Each party then strives to maximize the cost for the other of continued conflict.

The choice between acceptance of the other's offer and continued conflict must be made on the basis of a comparison between the anticipated cost of conflict for the period that it is expected to last and the anticipated difference between the current offer and the settlement that is expected to result from the conflict, a difference which will last for the life of the new contract. The greater the cost of conflict and the smaller the potential gain from conflict, the stronger is the incentive to accept the other's offer. There are two ways in which each party can increase the incentive for the other to accept.[7]

The first is by revising one's own offer in order to make it more attractive. The higher is the wage offered by the employer, the smaller is the further gain the union may expect to achieve by continued conflict. The lower is the wage at which the employees offer to continue to work, the smaller is the potential gain to the employer from continued conflict. If both parties revise their offers in an attempt to persuade the other to accept, the difference between the offers narrows. That difference is the maximum possible gain to each party from continued conflict. As the difference narrows, both parties become more reluctant to incur the cost of intensified conflict and more willing to make further concessions in an effort to reach agreement. If agreement is eventually achieved, the process of negotiation has worked and a new contract is signed.

Negotiation may well fail to result in agreement, however. As the difference between offers narrows, each party becomes more willing to accept the other's offer than to continue or intensify the conflict. But each knows that the other would rather yield than fight. Each may then refuse to give way in the expectation that the other will. If each is convinced that the other is about to accept, neither will. Each may then attempt to force the other to yield by increasing the cost for the other of continued conflict. Increasing the cost for the other is the second way in which each party can increase the incentive for the other to accept.

The objective for each party now is to impose costs or penalties on the other for refusing to accept, while minimizing the cost of conflict for itself. However detailed the contract of employment, current practice may well involve concessions by each party that are not contractual rights. These concessions may be withdrawn. Employees may "work to rule," for example, strictly observing the formal requirements of the job and stopping all variants or extensions thereof that have become common practice. The consequence is reduced productivity, which imposes costs on the employer, while the employees continue to be entitled to their normal wages. In retaliation the employer may withdraw various concessions commonly granted to employees that are not contractual rights.

When the current contract expires and negotiation has failed to achieve agreement on a new contract, employment may be suspended at the option of either party. The workers may strike or the employer impose a "lock-out." The employees then suffer the loss of their normal earnings less any support they may receive during the strike. The cost to the employer will depend on how crucial the group of employees are to the operation of the firm. If, for example, the only workers on strike are painters, gardeners, or others who perform routine maintenance or tasks peripheral to the operation of the firm, then production may continue with little difficulty for some time.

If, however, the strike includes workers without whom production cannot continue, the cost to the firm may be complete shut down. The more crucial are the workers to the continued operation of the firm, the greater is their power to impose costs on the employer by striking. Either party may increase the cost of conflict to the other by involving third parties. The employer may suspend employment by "laying-off" complementary groups of workers in order to bring pressure on the strikers not to inflict hardship on their friends by prolonging the dispute. The strikers may persuade other workers to respect their picket lines so as further to disrupt the operation of the firm, or may appeal to customers to boycott the firm's products.[8]

The work stoppage ends and production resumes when the parties reach agreement. As the costs of conflict continue and mount, each party finds that it is imposing costs on itself as well as on the other. There is then incentive to return to the technique of persuading the other party to end the conflict by making it a more favourable offer. The eventual agreement is typically between the offers of the parties at the beginning of the stoppage. Each can then claim victory and blame the other for an unnecessary dispute. When the public at large is seriously inconvenienced by the stoppage, government may intervene with legislation requiring compulsory arbitration. The parties themselves may agree on binding arbitration or, if one party favours that solution while the other does not, the former may wield political pressure on the government to intervene. On rare occasions none of these outcomes ensues and the breakdown becomes permanent, either because the firm goes out of business or finds some way to continue production without the workers in question, or because the workers individually find other jobs.

It is now time to consider how far the determination of wage rates by collective bargaining, with the occasional stoppage of work by reason of strike or lock-out, satisfies our three criteria of efficiency, equity, and integrity.

Efficiency

The process of bargaining itself involves costs regardless of the outcome. Both parties incur the costs of research in assembling the relevant data that constitute the information on which their offers are based. Bargaining is time consuming and both parties suffer uncertainty about the eventual outcome. But if the negotiations lead smoothly to an agreement, these costs need not be excessive. If each party uses only the first technique of bargaining, namely to make its own offer sufficiently attractive for the other to accept rather than incur the costs of conflict, and the series of offers converges to an agreement, the process is reasonably efficient. But if the parties have recourse to the second technique and deliberately impose costs of conflict on each other, then the process becomes inefficient, for resources are now devoted to generating costs. The degree of inefficiency will depend on the extent to which this technique is used. Bargaining and the necessary research that precedes it involve costs whether the bargaining is undertaken by individuals or collectively. Unions achieve an economy of scale, for the same research and negotiation serve all workers. But the major inefficiency costs arise only when the second technique is used, and that typically happens only with collective bargaining.

Working to rule is the deliberate adoption of inefficient work methods rather than the more efficient procedures that have become the normal practice. The inefficiency of the bargaining process increases enormously when work is stopped, whether because of a strike or lock-out. When work stops, labour ceases producing and the product is lost to society. The workers suffer the loss of wages and the sudden withdrawal of labour also forces complementary factors to be idle. Machines cannot function without workers to operate them and the services of capital are lost. Other workers in the firm may be unable to produce in the absence of the group in question and they become idle too. Materials cannot be processed without people to process them and suppliers of materials to the firm in question may become idle. Those who work with the products of the firm may be unable to function without them and their contribution to the output of society is also lost.[9]

The modern economy is based on a complex set of interdependence relationships. When one part of the system stops working, other parts may be unable to continue. No person or group is irreplaceable, but some are indispensable. When their services are lost, the cost may be very high indeed until they are replaced and arranging replacement takes time. During a temporary work stoppage permanent replacement is not worthwhile and whatever temporary substitution is possible may still involve much higher cost and lower efficiency. It is, of course, precisely because the employer depends on the work in question, and the workers depend on their jobs, that a work stoppage caused by one party imposes costs on the other. That is the intended purpose of a strike or lock-out.

The temporary withdrawal of labour or employment differs from permanent withdrawal in two ways. First, if one worker resigns from a job, the employer incurs costs of search and training. If he is dismissed, the worker incurs costs of search and mobility. The purpose of liquidated damages for termination of employment by either party is to force the one terminating the employment to compensate the other. The one who withdraws then meets the costs of withdrawal. But no liquidated damages are paid when work is suspended temporarily by a strike or lock-out. The essential feature of the strike or lock-out is that the party who withdraws from the employment relationship inflicts costs on the other. The second difference between temporary and permanent withdrawal is that it is much easier to replace one worker than all workers of a particular type in a firm. When one employee resigns, either his colleagues must continue without him or a new member must be found and added to the team. Continuing workers train the new recruit. But when all workers strike together, the entire production process may stop. If the work stoppage is predicted, both parties may prepare for it in order to minimize the costs. The employer may accumulate inventories of the product and workers may accumulate personal savings and plan to make use of the time off work by, for example, painting their houses or taking vacations. To the extent that neither party suffers, however, the work stoppage fails to serve its purpose. It is only when costs are incurred that the parties feel pres-sure to reach agreement.

The interdependence of individuals in an economy arises because each performs a function that benefits others. The exchange of services is the essence of the efficiency of the system. In the conflict phase of collective bargaining, however, each party devotes time and effort to behaving in a way that will inflict harm on the other, though each will try to avoid consequences harmful to itself. Striking workers may permit essential maintenance of the plant to continue because they do not wish to destroy the basis of their future employment. The employer may refrain from hiring substitute labour because it does not wish to worsen future relations with its employees. The expectation that employment will resume is the essential feature of the indefinite period contract. As in boxing, the rules of the game permit black eyes and bloody noses, but not blows below the belt. The essential purpose of the strike and lock-out is to inflict costs on the other, however, for that is the only way to coerce the other party to settle. The use of resources to generate costs is the antithesis of efficiency.

If the two parties to the dispute were the only ones who suffered from it, the consequent inefficiency would be contained. Others would not have a direct interest. It may then be argued that the two parties are together responsible for their own misfortunes, for they choose to fight rather than co-operate in reaching agreement, and the rest of society should adopt the attitude of disinterested spectators. But this is not the attitude that society adopts to private feuds between individuals in other contexts. A society governed by the rule of law does not turn a blind eye to conflict between neighbours over trivial disputes. Argument is tolerated, but when each begins deliberately to inflict costs on the other, the stage is reached at which society as a whole invokes the process of law to terminate the fight and arbitrate the issue. Either party may seek police protection from the harmful acts of the other, and seek redress from the courts in either the law of tort or contract as may be appropriate. But even when neither party desires the intervention of third parties, the society still intervenes when the potential harm to the parties exceeds the tolerated limits of private dispute. Duelling is illegal even though the only persons involved are the two who want to duel. Society as a whole has a similar interest when two parties deliberately inflict costs on each other by conflict in the process of collective bargaining. The inefficiency of conflict is a matter of social concern when only the parties to the conflict suffer. That concern grows when third parties are also adversely affected. The public interest in the efficiency of the collective bargaining process is the subject of the next chapter.

The process of collective bargaining may be either reasonably efficient if negotiation leads smoothly to agreement, or very inefficient if costly conflict occurs. The outcome of the process must be assessed separately in terms of its efficiency. The characteristics of an efficient labour market were discussed in chapter 2. They were that labour should be fully utilized; that it should be optimally allocated among tasks, each worker performing the task that is most highly valued in the society; that there should be incentive for optimal effort; and that there should be an optimal degree of mobility. The outcome of the collective bargaining process is a wage rate for each job and the question is whether those wage rates are conducive to the achievement of efficiency.

Markets based on individual contracts work by marginal adjustments. Individuals decide to buy or sell one more or one less unit of a good or service at current prices and equilibrium prices adjust to balance desires to buy and sell in each market. Collective bargaining, however, is not a marginal process. The wage rate is determined by negotiation for the entire current group of workers involved and that wage is then fixed for the life of the contract. Decisions to expand or contract the number of employees do not affect the wage rate during the life of the contract, nor is the wage rate for a new contract determined entirely by excess supply or demand in the market. The wage rate resulting from bargaining can be anywhere in the range bounded by the maximum the employer would be willing to pay rather than lose the entire group of workers and the minimum the workers would accept rather than lose their jobs. The wage rate may then be too high or too low from the standpoint of economic efficiency. The wage is too high if it deters employers from employing workers who would be willing and able to work for less. It is too low if it is less than the value consumers place on the marginal product of labour. Wage rates that are either too high or too low encourage suboptimal use of labour.

Collective bargaining typically results in higher wages than would exist without it, for when first introduced it normally replaces unfettered power by the employer to set wage rates. A weak union, however, may achieve little improvement over the previous situation. It is quite possible for wage rates set by collective bargaining to be too low from the standpoint of efficiency even though they are not as low as would prevail in the absence of collective bargaining.

If the wage rate is too low, employers will find it profitable to employ an excessive number of workers and use labour-intensive techniques of production. Their intentions may, however, be frustrated by a shortage of labour. Expansion that would be profitable at current wage rates will not be possible unless additional labour can be recruited. This will prove expensive for the individual firm and impossible for all firms together since the very fact that the wage rate is too low implies that the demand for labour exceeds the supply. The tendency to invest to an excessive extent in capital that is

complementary to cheap labour rather than in capital that substitutes for labour will also be curtailed by the difficulty of
increasing employment. Since employers will not compete for
scarce labour by competitive wage rate increases, there is no
reason to suppose that labour will be allocated optimally among
firms. Existing workers will not receive adequately attractive
offers to persuade them to change employment to a task more
highly valued by society and there will be too low a degree
of labour mobility. Low wages also mean that the incentive
to work at all, and to devote optimal effort to the job if employed, will be too weak. The essential problem of wage rates
that are too low is that the wage is less than the value customers place on the product of labour. There is full employment, but the labour force is not most efficiently employed.
These problems were discussed earlier as the consequences of
a system in which wage rates are set by employers, the case
in which employers have total power to set wage rates being
the extreme case of a system of collective bargaining in which
the balance of power rests entirely with the employer.

If the wage rate resulting from collective bargaining is too
high, there is also inefficiency in the labour market.[10] Employers then find it profitable to economize excessively in the
employment of labour. Too few workers are employed. The
total demand for labour is less than the available supply and
labour is not fully utilized. This dimension of inefficiency manifests itself as a high rate of unemployment.[11] The contractual
fixing of the wage rate in each firm prevents the unemployed
from competing for jobs by offering their services at less than
the prevailing wage rate. The high cost of labour for the firm
creates an incentive to employ capital-intensive techniques of
production and to invest in capital that substitutes for labour
rather than capital complementary to labour that would expand the level of employment.[12] When those without jobs cannot secure an offer of employment, while those with jobs are
bound by a fixed wage rate and protected by high liquidated
damages for dismissal, there is little incentive for either group
to devote optimal effort to work. The efficiency of the allocation of labour among firms and the optimal degree of mobility
among jobs are, however, matters of little concern while surplus labour is unemployed. The major concern from the standpoint of efficiency is that labour is underutilized and there is
inefficient allocation and inefficient mobility between work and
idleness.

Since each group of workers in the economy negotiates separately under a system of collective bargaining, and not all wage rates are determined by collective bargaining, it is very likely that wage rates will simultaneously be too high in some occupations and too low in others. This situation can arise whether collective bargaining is practised by only part of the labour force or by virtually the entire labour force. When only part of the labour force is covered we should typically expect wage rates to be high in the unionized sector relative to the nonunionized sector. If the entire labour market were governed by collective bargaining, we should still expect some unions in some occupations to be more successful than others in achieving high wages – wage rates in some occupations will be high relative to others. There are problems of efficiency if wage rates are on the whole too high or too low, and there are further problems if some are too high relative to others.

When wage rates in some occupations are too high relative to others the result will be inefficient allocation of labour among jobs. Too few will be employed in jobs where the wage rate is too high, and the incentive there will be to invest excessively in labour-substituting rather than employment-creating capital. Too many workers will then be forced to seek employment elsewhere, which may result in very low wage rates in markets that approximate perfect competition.[13] If such low wage rates persuade governments to impose a minimum wage above the competitive level, then the surplus labour will not be absorbed in low wage occupations and the consequence will be excessive unemployment.

Collective bargaining can result in wage rates that are much too high or much too low only if the range of possible outcomes is wide. That range reflects the costs of search, training, and mobility. In a market in which wages are determined by separate negotiation with each worker, the costs of search and training govern the extent to which the employer would be prepared to pay an existing worker more than he would have to pay for a replacement. The costs of search and mobility similarly determine the extent to which the worker would accept a wage lower than he could earn in a different job. Both these measures rely on the availability of other workers and other jobs. If collective bargaining is the common practice, however, the alternative ceases to be available. The wage rate fixed by the agreement is the wage that the employer would have to pay for either retention of the current employee or for a replacement worker. The relevant maximum is no longer set by a search and training cost premium over the "market wage" for a single new recruit, but by the maximum that would be paid rather than lose the services of the entire group of current employees. That maximum is not unbounded, for closure or complete reorganization of the firm would be preferred to a wage rate so high that it would inevitably result in high losses and eventual bankruptcy. But it is much higher than the maximum that would prevail with individual bargaining. When there is unemployment and alternative jobs for the workers are in occupations similarly subject to collective bargaining, the worker has little prospect of attractive employment and his reservation wage is correspondingly low. Thus the range of possible collective bargaining outcomes widens the more widespread the practice of collective bargaining. There is then certainly scope for wage rates that are inefficiently high or inefficiently low to a significant extent.

There is in the collective bargaining process no automatic mechanism tending to correct wage rates that are inefficiently high or inefficiently low. If the current contract specifies a wage rate already inefficiently high, a new agreement calling for a still higher wage rate may result in the firm reducing the size of its labour force. Fear of this consequence may deter the union from bargaining for a higher wage unless it can protect itself from the threatened consequences. Two forms of protection, however, are available. The union may bargain for a clause in the contract that would require the employer to select workers for lay-off in an agreed way. Typically either the last hired is the first to go, or the oldest workers are retired early. If the employer is indifferent about which workers to release, such a clause may be secured by the union at little cost. The vast majority of union members are then secure in their jobs and can use their majority power to require the union to bargain hard for increased wages.[14] Even stronger protection from lay-off would be secured by a clause guaranteeing job security for all existing workers. The employer will be more reluctant to agree to this, for a reduction in the labour force could then be achieved only by attrition, but may agree in exchange for some concession on the extent of the increased wage sought. Although both techniques reduce the employment of new recruits, and the former may even result in some recent recruits being returned to the ranks of the unemployed, they do not prevent a further increase in a wage rate that is already inefficiently high.[15]

When bargaining is only about the wage rate, and the wage rate that results is above the efficient level, it is inevitably true that more workers want jobs than the employer finds it profitable to employ. Therein lies the inherent inefficiency of the exercise of monopoly power. If the union is concerned about the plight of excluded workers, there is then scope for an alternative contract that would leave both the employer and the union in preferred positions. Such a contract would specify a lower wage rate and also a minimum guaranteed level of employment. Guaranteed minimum employment can be expressed in terms of the total number of workers to be employed or in terms of job security for existing workers who are guaranteed employment for a specified minimum number of weeks per year. Such contracts are sometimes called "efficient contracts" for if optimally designed they satisfy the *paretian* criteria discussed in chapter 2: both parties are better off than if only the wage rate were specified and it would not be possible to define conditions that would leave both parties still better off. It does not follow, however, that "efficient contracts" are efficient when considered in a broader context.

The welfare of many parties is affected by the terms of an employment contract. The employer's interest is directly represented in the negotiations and the union represents the interests of existing workers. From the standpoint of these two parties, "efficient" contracts are efficient. But potential workers not currently employed are not represented by the union, and no one represents the interests of customers for the product or suppliers of other factors of production. The firm may negotiate contracts with other suppliers that are efficient in the same sense as the "efficient" contract of employment. Lower prices may be specified in exchange for guaranteed minimum volumes of purchases. But no such collectively negotiated contracts are possible with potential workers or consumers. If such contracts were possible, still greater efficiency could be achieved and all parties could be better off. This follows from the fact that excluded workers would be willing to work for a slightly lower wage rate and excluded customers to buy the extra product for a slightly lower price. But without scope for efficient contracts, and in the absence of feasible wage and price discrimination, the excluded are not accommodated.

An "efficient" employment contract is more efficient for all concerned than a contract specifying only a wage rate that is too high. Both parties agree to it, more workers are employed, more of other factors of production are used, and more of the product is produced so that it has to be sold at a lower price. But the contract is still inefficient from the standpoint of society as a whole, whereas a contract specifying an efficient wage is efficient in both the narrow and broader senses. If the wage rate is efficient, there is no need to specify the level of employment because the number of qualified persons wanting jobs will be equal to the number the employer finds it profitable to employ. Thus, the inclusion of a clause in a contract specifying a minimum level of employment, while indicating that the contract is more efficient than it would be without such a clause, is itself evidence that the wage rate is too high from the standpoint of efficiency for the economy as a whole. "Efficient contracts" are efficient only in the sense that the employer and the union are co-operating efficiently to exploit other groups.

In theory there is symmetrical scope for "efficient contracts" when the wage rate is too low. But in this case the employer would want to employ more workers than are willing to work and the guaranteed employment clause would have to be a promise that workers would be available. Since the union could not ensure the availability of workers, in practice "efficient contracts" do not arise in this case. If the wage rate is already inefficiently low, the employer may fear that some workers will voluntarily leave his employment. He may then bargain for clauses that increase the liquidated damages for resignation. Again we find that as the wage becomes too high or too low the tendency is not for a self-correcting wage rate but for supplementary measures that widen the bargaining range. In a labour market characterized by collective bargaining, the individual participants do not confront incentives to reverse any tendency for the wage rate to be either inefficiently high or inefficiently low.

The common defence of collective bargaining is that due process of bargaining with balanced power is more equitable than the possible exploitation of individual workers by a powerful employer. When collective bargaining begins for an occupational group, it typically replaces a situation in which the wage rate is set by the employer. It was argued above that the ability of the employer to set the wage rate may result in his expropriating the entire margin of rent: committed workers are exploited and the wage rate is inequitably low. Collective bargaining, it is argued, results in a balance of power that redresses that inequity. We must now ask how far the system of collective bargaining is likely to be equitable, examining first the process and then the outcome.

Equity

At first glance the process of collective bargaining appears equitable as far as the parties to the negotiations are concerned. Each is comparably free to make and revise offers, to accept or reject the other's offer, and to negotiate towards an agreement. But this simple view ignores many of the issues of equity involved. The contract being negotiated will govern the conditions of employment of many individual workers. Each in principle is a self-proprietor of his own human capital. If the decision to form a union and bargain collectively is unanimous, then no worker's rights are violated. But unanimity is rare. Some workers may oppose formation of the union and may oppose the policies of the union once formed, even though those policies are endorsed by majority vote. The individual worker loses his right to negotiate the conditions of the sale of his own labour and is instead bound by the decision of the group. It may well be argued that if the choice is between an offer set by the employer and an offer achieved by collective bargaining, which the individual is free in either event only to accept or reject, then he has no individual bargaining power in either case and is likely to receive the better offer from the collective bargaining process. But this argument is not necessarily valid. The individual worker may be willing to continue to work and the employer be willing to continue to employ him at the current wage rate, yet a higher wage rate secured by collective bargaining may result in reduction of the labour force and lay-off of the individual. In that case the individual has clearly suffered from a process that denies him the right to accept a lower wage offer.

Equity among workers in a particular union may be presumed to exist when all are governed by the same contract. But when the contract specifies seniority differentials or job differentials different from those that would have prevailed in the absence of collective bargaining, the respective interests of different workers are clearly at issue and it is an open question which process is more equitable.[16]

When the process of bargaining breaks down and there is a strike or lock-out, the individual is temporarily denied the option to accept the employer's offer. An employee who would rather accept that offer than suffer the consequences of a work stoppage has clearly lost his individual right to contract the sale of his own labour. Majority rule within the union may well mean that the rights of individuals are overridden and this may be considered inequitable.

Although all workers in the same union are governed by the same negotiations, workers in different unions, or involved in negotiations with different employers, may well have different degrees of power in the negotiation process and such differences may be inequitable. A small group of workers whose services are indispensable to the continuing operation of the entire firm, whose total wages are small in relation to the total costs of the firm, and whose employer could readily pass on the cost of higher wages by charging customers higher prices, are clearly in a strong bargaining position. A group of workers whose services could be dispensed with temporarily without great inconvenience, a large group whose total wages are a very high proportion of the firm's total costs, or a group whose employer could not increase prices because of foreign competition, will be in a weaker bargaining position. There is no reason to consider such differences in bargaining strength to be equitable. In a competitive labour market workers earn wages in relation to the value of their services to society. Under collective bargaining their relative wages may more reflect their ability to threaten to disrupt the functioning of society. It may be questioned whether competitive wages result in an equitable distribution of income, but it is even more questionable whether the distribution of income according to the power to inflict damage on society is equitable.

The parties to the process of collective bargaining are the employer and the union representing the employees. But they are not the only parties with an interest in the process. Suppliers to the firm in question, employees who work with the members of the union in question, and customers who buy the product of the firm all have an interest in smooth negotiations with no work stoppage or slowdown that may adversely affect them. If a number of firms exist in an industry, suppliers and customers will tend to avoid dealing with firms that acquire a reputation for unreliability because of repeated work stoppages. But when all are governed by collective bargaining, it may be impossible to predict where disputes will arise. Other parties cannot avoid the risk that their normal operations will be disrupted by a strike over which they have no control. Although they have an interest in avoiding the stoppage and resolving any dispute speedily, they have no voice in the proceedings and are not represented in the bargaining. Only if government intervenes to require compulsory arbitration are the interests of such third parties in any way represented. The distribution of power to influence a process that can have very serious consequences for many people is not equitable if none but the immediate participants has any power at all.

The outcome of the collective bargaining process is a set of negotiated wage rates. There is in principle no reason to suppose that these will be equitable in any sense. The relative wages of different groups of workers will reflect their bargaining strength, which may bear little resemblance to the value of their services to society. The bargaining strength of a union relies in the last resort on the damage it can inflict by a temporary withdrawal of its services. In cases where there are neither inventories nor substitutes that damage can be severe. But it does not follow that the value of a service on a long-run continuing basis is related to the urgency of its short-run availability. Coal and oil can be stored, electricity cannot. A strike that interrupts production in the coal mines or oil fields for a day would be far less serious in it consequences than one that closes power stations, but this does not mean that coal miners and oil field workers should have less bargaining power than workers in power stations. The importance of different services is not necessarily related to their urgency. Educational services are less urgent then medical services, but not less important. Equitable wage differences among occupations reflect the forces of supply and demand in those occupations. High training costs, rare native abilities, and arduous, dangerous, or unpleasant work result in high wages, but they are not necessarily reflected in great bargaining strength in the short-run context of wage negotiations.

Wage rates determined in the immediate heat of conflict are then fixed by contract for a defined period. Other members of the labour force may well be willing and able to perform the work in question for a lower wage rate, but are denied the opportunity to compete. Members of unions with great bargaining strength are thus afforded an inequitable power to exploit the rest of society.[17] High wages are reflected in high prices and the consumer is exploited. More serious is the exclusion of other potential workers from the opportunity to sell their services. If the wage rate is too high, the product price is too high, the level of employment and output is too low, and investment is concentrated on labour-saving rather than employment-generating capital. Other workers are inequitably excluded from occupations in which they could provide their most valuable contribution to society. This problem was discussed above in the context of efficiency, but a system that prevents workers from performing services at wage rates that would lead to prices that customers would be willing to pay also inflicts inequity on the excluded workers and customers. Frustrated workers must instead enter other occupations, which increases supply and reduces wage rates there, or remain unemployed living on inequitably low incomes that must be met by inequitably high taxes on society as a whole. Yet neither the union nor the firm in an industry where wages are too high has both the incentive and the power to modify wage rates to reflect the inequitable consequences of the exercise of bargaining power.

The system of collective bargaining may be more equitable as far as the workers and employer in a particular contract are concerned than a system in which the employer has sole power to set the wage rate. But a society characterized by collective bargaining that results in inefficiently high wages in some occupations, inefficiently low wages in others, and no wages at all for those excluded from the labour market and consigned to unemployment, is far from equitable from the standpoint of society as a whole.

Integrity

The third criterion, integrity, can also be considered with respect to both the process and the outcome of collective bargaining. The indefinite period contract with periodic renegotiation of the wage rate gives rise to a basic problem of integrity when both parties are committed to continuation of the contract with no precise specification of the terms of the continuing contract to which they are committed. The common understanding is that the wage rate will be renegotiated periodically. Integrity is not violated if the parties negotiate in good faith in ways that both implicitly agreed would be reasonable, but there is a breach of integrity when tactics are used that were no part of the initial contract. The purpose of liquidated damages is to compensate one party for default by the other. The employee, for example, may rely on security of his income protected by the promise of notice, or payment in lieu thereof, if employment is terminated. If his employment subsequently becomes subject to collective bargaining, however, he may be subject to temporary suspension of employment by lock-out with no compensation. The employer similarly enjoys security of his workforce protected by the liquidated damages that accrue when an employee terminates the contract. A strike, however, provides no such compensation. Such breaches of integrity arise only on the introduction of collective bargaining. There is no breach of integrity when both parties agree to the process of bargaining that both know may lead to strike or lock-out.

Just as the parties to a contract of employment become committed to continuation of the contract, so do the parties to other contracts. The firm depends on continuation of the contractual arrangements by which it receives supplies of factors and sells its product. When one firm stops production because of a strike or lock-out, both those supplying it and those receiving its product are confronted with a breakdown of the contracts on which they rely. Their reasonable expectations are violated whether or not contractual commitments are broken. The customer who commits himself to a single source of supply of a product or service, on the promise that supply will continue uninterrupted, may find that promise broken. Such breaches of integrity with third parties are particularly important in the case of monopolies, for substitute sources of supply do not exist. The citizen dependent on gas or electricity supply, on the post office for communication, on health or fire protection services – industries either operated or regulated by government – enjoys an implicit commitment that such services will be available continuously. Interruption of service by reason of strike or lock-out then constitutes a breach of integrity. Thus just as the criteria of efficiency and equity must be considered with respect to the impact that the collective bargaining process may have on third parties, as well as on the employer and employee, so must the criterion of integrity.

The outcome of the collective bargaining process also raises severe problems of integrity for third parties, although the honouring of a contract once made would involve no breach of integrity for the parties to the contract. In a market economy the individual depends on markets for survival. The person who owns only his own labour cannot be self-sufficient. He must either sell the services of his labour or live on charity. Essential to the social contract that implicitly underlies the market economy is the right of access to markets. The person who desires to enter the labour market as an employee must offer his services on terms that some employer is willing to accept. While he cannot enter professions or skilled trades for which he lacks the required qualifications, he does have the implicit right to compete for employment in submarkets where he has skills and abilities comparable with those currently employed. A free labour market does not have a predetermined level of employment. The lower the wage rate the more workers are employers willing to employ. If new entrants to the labour market cannot find jobs at current wage rates, the excess supply of labour in the submarkets for which they are qualified should cause a fall in the wage rate and increase in the number of jobs. The new entrant essentially auctions his services, offering to work for lower and lower wages until he finds an employer willing to employ him. This is the only way in which a market can work. If it does not work in this way, and cannot be made to work in this or any other way, then the market does not work to accommodate those willing to sell their services.

When the wage rate is determined by collective bargaining it does not fall to accommodate potential new entrants to the occupation. Those currently employed succeed in maintaining or increasing their wage rate by excluding others from the right to compete. The case of a wage that is too high was discussed above as violating the principles of efficiency and equity. It also violates integrity by excluding the new entrant from his right to enter the market.

New entrants unable to find employment at current wage rates because employers already have all the workers they consider it profitable to employ at current wage rates, are restricted to those submarkets in which they can compete by offering to work for lower wage rates. If a legislated minimum wage prohibits their offering their services for less than the specified minimum wage, then they may be totally excluded from the labour market. Persons excluded from high wage jobs seek lower wage employment, forcing those who would normally find low wage jobs to seek still lower wage jobs. When the floor of the minimum wage is reached, those still seeking employment are excluded altogether. The hardest hit are new entrants to the labour force with little education, no skills, and no experience.[18] A significant proportion of young entrants to the labour market are in fact excluded in this way and consigned to unemployment, surviving on subsistence allowances charitably provided at taxpayers' expense. Their exclusion denies them the rights of access to the labour market, which is a serious breach of integrity with respect to an essential promise implicit in the social contract of a market society. The right to sell labour services is restricted in many ways in modern society, but usually for good reason and with appropriate alternatives. Children are prohibited from working in factories when they should be in school and society provides for the schools and the sustenance of children. Some occupations are prohibited and others discouraged because they are considered socially undesirable. Persons who would enter such occupations if free to do so are encouraged and helped to find socially desirable employment instead. The combination of collective bargaining and minimum wage laws, however, may deny adults the right to enter socially desirable occupations at market wage rates while providing no alternative other than crime or poverty and the stigma of idleness and social charity.

In a market system the individual has a symmetrical right to offer to buy goods and services at prices that would make it profitable to employ workers to produce them at wage rates for which they would be willing to work. Exclusion of a significant proportion of the labour force from the labour market implies exclusion of potential customers from the market for their products. Failure to achieve full utilization of the labour force is an important characteristic of an inefficient labour market, and it implies both inequity and breach of integrity with respect to frustrated potential workers and consumers.

In the discussion so far I have focused on the direct participants in the labour market, with some discussion of the interest of third parties. In the next chapter I focus on the public interest and in the following chapter, the labour market in the public sector.

CHAPTER FIVE

The Public Interest

"The public interest" is a widely used and often vaguely defined term. It will be used here to refer to the interest that members of society have in the consequences of alternative structures of the labour market. Clearly the participants themselves have a crucial interest in the way a market operates. The public interest refers to the consequences for people other than the immediate participants. To say that something is of interest to the public means that it affects third parties to a significant extent whether beneficially or harmfully. The effects may be so widespread that virtually every citizen is affected, or they may be concentrated on particular segments of society. The public interest is important whenever a significant number of people are affected to a significant extent by events that they do not have the power either to control or influence.[1]

The principle of the self-proprietorship of human capital discussed in chapter 2 is closely associated with the idea of individual freedom and the right freely to negotiate the sale of the services of one's own labour. These principles of freedom are often extended to defend the right to bargain collectively and to withdraw services collectively by strike action. Before all such freedoms are accepted as sacrosanct, however, we must ask why our society adopted and maintains an economic system based on free markets.

The principles of freedom of the individual, freedom to produce and exchange, and freedom to enjoy the fruits of one's own labour have deep roots in western philosophy. But they became the foundation of an economic system based on free markets not only because of their inherent rightness but also because economic reasoning demonstrated that adoption of a free market system would be expedient in the service of the public interest.[2] Since the late eighteenth century economists have been concerned with the theoretical proposition that competitive free markets achieve an efficient equilibrium. That was the case for *laissez-faire*. It was no part of that case that individuals should be free to affect others adversely. *Laissez-faire* did not mean anarchy, and freedom did not mean freedom to wield power in one's own interest at the expense of others. Freedom to exchange did not mean freedom to exploit. Economists demonstrated that under certain circumstances the private and public interest would coincide and freedom of economic behaviour would be an efficient system. Under other circumstances, the private and public interest would not coincide and constraints on freedom would be needed. A brief review of those different sets of circumstances will help to place the system of collective bargaining in proper perspective.

The private and public interest coincide in perfectly competitive markets for purely private goods. Each individual must control such a small part of the total stock or flow of goods and services that he is powerless to affect any price. Individuals can control only quantities, not prices, and each can control such a small proportion of the total quantity that he can make only marginal adjustments to the system as a whole. Such marginal adjustments are matters of no concern to the public at large. The theory demonstrates that when each individual adjusts his own affairs in the pursuit of his private interest, the total effect of such adjustments serves the public interest. It is then in the public interest to permit freedom of individual economic behaviour.

The outcome is quite different when a single individual, or a small group, controls such a large quantity of a particular good or service that adjustment of that quantity will significantly affect the price. There is then private incentive for sellers to reduce supply in order to increase price, and for buyers to reduce demand in order to decrease price. In either event the total quantity produced and sold is less than the quantity that would be most efficient or would best serve the public interest. Such cases have received most attention in the context of monopoly or oligopoly, when there is only one or few sellers, though symmetrical cases arise when there is only one or a few buyers. Since competition serves the public interest, the restraint of competition is detrimental to the public interest. It is always in the private interest of a seller to prevent others from selling similar goods, and of a buyer to prevent others from buying them. In a perfectly competitive market no person has the power to restrict competition. When that power is present the private and public interest no longer coincide.

Perfectly competitive markets work by separate determination of the prices of quantities of a good or service that are small in relation to the total. Competition then forces the resulting prices to converge to an equilibrium. Individuals, although free to bargain, are powerless to maintain prices above or below that equilibrium. At the equilibrium price the total quantity produced and sold is maximized, for if prices were higher there would be a shortage of buyers and if lower, a shortage of sellers. With collective bargaining, or bilateral monopoly, a single price is negotiated for the entire quantity produced. There is then no reason to suppose that the negotiated price will optimally serve the public interest. If it is either above or below the competitive equilibrium level the total quantity produced will be less than the most efficient amount.

An extreme system of *laissez-faire* fails to serve the public interest when the conditions that lead to coincidence of the private and public interest are not satisfied. Public goods are not provided, except by charitable organizations, for it is in no one's interest to provide them, and goods produced in markets characterized by monopoly are not produced in sufficient quantity. The opposite extreme case of state control of economic activity, however, incurs unnecessary administrative costs in regulating less than perfectly those markets that would serve the public interest optimally if left free. Our own society has evolved a system that is not governed by adherence to philosophical principles concerning the proper means of organizing economic activity, but by the pragmatic selection of means best suited to serve the public interest. We are not doctrinaire libertarians, but permit free enterprise to flourish wherever conditions are such that the private and public interest coincide. We are not doctrinaire socialists, but use state control of economic activity whenever it appears to serve the public interest to do so. Public goods are provided in the public sector. Natural monopolies are either operated by government or regulated by government. Each case is resolved on an *ad hoc* basis by the principle of expediency, and there is continuous debate concerning the best approach to individual cases.

The labour market poses a dilemma. It is of crucial importance that the labour market should function well, for it organizes the allocation of human effort in economic activity and provides the major source of income for the bulk of the population. We abhor slavery and the compulsory direction of labour and endeavour to leave individuals as free as possible to control the use of their own productive activities. But the *laissez-faire* approach to the labour market is not tolerable because the market is not characterized by the conditions of perfect competition that would bring about coincidence of the private and public interest. In much of the economy the efficient size of the production unit is large. Big firms employ many people and would accordingly have power to set wage rates and exploit workers. Mobility is costly and the forces of competition weak. Yet state control of the labour market would imply direction of workers and control of employers, which would place virtually all economic activity under state control. A third system has evolved in which the power of the employer is confronted by the consolidated power of workers organized into a union. Balanced conflict, however, is very different from either free competition or state control. The hope has been that if the parties are reasonably well matched in power, the outcome will be a reasonable compromise. The rules of conflict are prescribed by legislation and the process is monitored. If disputes become bitter, there is provision for mediation or conciliation. In the last resort, if a dispute threatens the public interest to an intolerable extent, the power of the state can be used on an *ad hoc* basis to impose compulsory arbitration. If the outcome of the process is that wage rates generally increase at such rate that they are perceived to be a cause of inflation, there is *ad hoc* recourse to guidelines or imposed wage controls.

State intervention to terminate particular disputes or control wages generally clearly indicates that the system is perceived politically to have failed to an intolerable extent to serve the public interest. Yet the system could continue to work badly and fail to serve the public interest optimally without such failure being considered sufficiently intolerable to warrant the draconian step of state intervention. The issue is whether the system of balanced conflict under the current rules of the game normally serves the public interest well, and if not, whether changes to the system can be devised that would make it work better. Before that question is addressed, we must be clear about what the public interest in the system is. Previous chapters have considered the criteria of efficiency, equity, and integrity. We can now ask whether the current system satisfies those criteria to an acceptable degree, and if not, how far the public interest is violated.

EFFICIENCY

The economic system is a social institution. It marshals and constrains the economic activities of all citizens. Each has the right to use the system in any legal way to further his private interest and all have the collective right to modify it in the public interest. Society as a whole accepts the obligation to ensure that each individual receives at least minimal sustenance and with that responsibility goes the right to ensure that resources are efficiently used. To the extent that there is a social responsibility to provide citizens with the products of labour, there is a social right to ensure that labour is employed efficiently to produce those products. To the extent that the individual bears responsibility for his own sustenance, there is an individual right to access to an efficient economic system. Ensuring that the economic system is efficient, and in particular that it results in the efficient use of labour, is both a social right and a social responsibility.

Labour is employed in the private sector by individual and institutional employers acting in their private interest, but ensuring that labour is employed efficiently is a social responsibility. The private and public interest can be reconciled by a labour market that ensures that employers are required to pay for the use of labour a wage that reflects the value of that labour to the society. The value of labour to the society is the value of the alternative use of that labour. No employer should be allowed to use labour for a wage less than the value of what that labour would otherwise produce. Nor should any employer be refused the right to use labour for a wage higher than its value in its current use. These conditions of efficiency are, of course, satisfied in a perfectly competitive market in equilibrium. The efficiency of any other system of wage determination can be assessed by examining the extent to which it satisfies the same conditions.

Once the wage rate for a particular type of labour has been determined, whether by market forces, collective bargaining, or regulation, each potential employer should have the right to employ such labour at that wage. If he is not able to find qualified workers after reasonable search at the prevailing wage or slightly above it, then the wage rate is too low, for current employers are being charged for that labour less than the amount at which the potential employer would value the services. If he is prevented from securing labour by offering a wage rate slightly above the prevailing rate, then the labour market is less than fully efficient. Whatever prevents him from competing effectively denies him access to the market and precludes an efficient allocation of labour.

The potential employee should have a similar right of access to the labour market. He should have the right to sell his labour at the prevailing wage for the skills he possesses. If he is unable after reasonable search to secure employment at the prevailing wage, and is prevented from finding employment by offering his services for a slightly lower wage, then he is denied the right to compete effectively. The prevailing wage rate is then inefficiently high, for it prevents employers from employing him at a wage rate that reflects the value he places on the alternative use of his time.

One valuable use of time is leisure, which can be defined as all time not spent in employment. So valuable is leisure that it absorbs most of the time of all persons who choose to work less than eighty-four hour weeks. In a labour market in which the individual is free to determine his own hours of work, he competes with employers for his own time, and reserves for his own use all hours that he values at more than the prevailing wage rate. Society also attaches value to leisure and achieves its objectives in a variety of ways. Various statutes have specified maximum hours of work, or minimum hours of leisure, have required that time be used for leisure on the sabbath and on statutory holidays, and have prohibited employment at wage rates below the social value of leisure. Minimum wage laws, in effect, specify a minimum value for leisure and prohibit employment at a wage rate less than the specified amount.

The efficient wage is equal to the social value of the alternative use of labour. That alternative use is either different employment or leisure. While different employment may not always be available as an alternative, leisure in the form of unemployment always is. Just as society as a whole is concerned if the system achieves too little leisure, so is it concerned if the system enforces too much. There is too much leisure for any unemployed individual who would prefer employment at the prevailing wage, or slightly less, in an occupation for which he has the required abilities and skills. His excess leisure in the form of enforced idleness is a matter of social concern if the employment he seeks would still leave him with the amount of leisure society requires. Compulsory excess leisure in this sense is the economist's definition of unemployment.

Social concern with excessive unemployment is concern about enforced leisure for the unemployed. When any individual is genuinely unemployed for more than the reasonable transitional time needed to search for an appropriate job, then it must be true that the prevailing wage for the job he seeks and is competent to perform is too high, for it is greater than the value of the alternative use of his time. That alternative is leisure and both he and society attach to his leisure a value less than the prevailing wage rate.

A dilemma for society exists when the only occupations for which the unemployed person is qualified are those in which the prevailing wage is the minimum wage, for logically society must then consider its own minimum wage to be too high. Minimum wage laws do not provide employment at the minimum wage, they only prohibit employment at wage rates below the specified minimum. Such laws are perfectly rational if society does attach to the leisure of the unemployment a value equal to the minimum wage. But the unemployment caused by the minimum wage is not then a social problem, for society places a value on the leisure of the unemployed equal to the value it would place on their employment at the minimum wage. Such unemployment could be a social problem only if society would prefer people to be employed at the minimum wage rather than remain unemployed, in which case society values their leisure at less than the minimum wage and that minimum is too high. A consistent society could have either a rational minimum wage law or a problem of unemployment, but according to the criterion of efficiency it cannot logically have both.

When a person is unable to secure employment at the prevailing wage, or slightly less, in an occupation for which he is qualified, he always has the option of unemployment. He may, however, also have the option of accepting employment in a lower wage occupation. Again it follows that the prevailing wage in the job he seeks is higher than the value of the alternative use of his time. By analogy with the concept of unemployment we can refer to such a person as "underemployed." Both unemployment and underemployment are symptoms of prevailing wage rates that are inefficiently high. Unemployment is a visible symptom, though the relevant definition differs from that used for statistics on unemployment, but underemployment is not visible and the extent of underemployment in the economy is difficult to assess.

The argument that unemployment is a symptom of inefficiently high wage rates has the corollary that if the relevant wage rates were lower there would be less unemployment. Such an argument would have been commonplace among economists in the nineteenth and early twentieth centuries. For a generation following the Great Depression of the 1930s, however, economists were obsessed with the macrodynamics of unemployment and with Keynesian theory in particular. That theory maintained that a market system may suffer from dynamic instability. If wage rates were perfectly flexible and instantly responsive to market pressures, they may be volatile. If wage rates were inflexible and currently at their long-run equilibrium levels, the level of employment may be volatile. The problem was perceived as one of inadequate or unstable aggregate demand and a solution was sought in fiscal policy designed to complement and stabilize the system. Unemployment was then attributed to deficient aggregate demand and did not necessarily indicate that wage rates were above long-run efficient levels.

The tragedy was that classical theory and Keynesian theory were perceived as rival explanations of the same phenomenon, yet they may be better viewed as complementary explanations of different phenomena in the same system. Macroeconomics is a complicated subject and much technical research and argument surrounds the controversies with which it is currently beset. I cannot do justice to the debate in this study and can at most present rather superficially the major relevant differences between the two schools of thought. Classical theory maintained that if real wage rates are too high and are prevented from falling, the consequence will be unemployment. Keynesian theory argued that unemployment can result from inadequate aggregate demand. Each theory may be valid in appropriate circumstances. The problem is to identify the cause of unemployment at a particular time.

For many years it was generally agreed that the Keynesian explanation of unemployment in the 1930s was valid. Given the belief that in depressions and recessions the level of unemployment rises for reasons that are better explained by Keynesian than classical theory, it was tempting to conclude that because Keynesian theory was valid, classical theory was not. A generation of economists succumbed to this temptation and attributed virtually all unemployment to inadequate aggregate demand. Yet there was nothing in Keynesian theory that refuted the basic validity of classical theory. If real wage rates, the real costs of employing labour, are too high and are prevented from falling, there will be unemployment. The policy of inflation as a cure for unemployment works in theory only if prices rise faster than wages so that real wage rates fall. If real wage rates do not fall, that policy does not work. When a high level of unemployment persists and real wage rates are maintained despite inflation, that unemployment is better explained by classical theory than by Keynesian.

The basic ideas of classical economics have been resurrected in recent years in what has come to be called the new classical macroeconomics.[3] The basic idea is that governmental intervention in the economy by monetary and fiscal policy will be successful only if it is not anticipated. The rational expectations hypothesis argues that any consistent government policy, or any policy rule that adjusts policy in a prescribed way to economic indicators, will be anticipated and accordingly ineffective. Well-organized unions are, of course, better able to anticipate policy than are individual workers, and better able to reflect those anticipations in negotiated wage rates. Rational expectations are therefore more powerful as a force in the system the greater the extent of unionization. The early success of Keynesian policy relied on its ability to take decision makers in the private sector by surprise. Once the element of surprise is lost, the policy ceases to be effective. The stable relationship is not between the rate of inflation and the unemployment rate, but between the rate of increase of real wage rates and the unemployment rate.[4] To the extent that inflation is anticipated, it has no effect on the level of employment. If any consistent policy to influence the inflation rate is expected, it can have no effect on the level of unemployment.

That the level of employment is negatively related to real wage rates, and accordingly to the rate of increase of real wage rates relative to the rate of increase in productivity, is simply the classical law of supply and demand. The recent rediscovery of that law by macroeconomists has led them to focus attention on one direction of the causal relationship. The higher the level of unemployment, the lower will be the rate of increase of real wage rates. That relationship explains why it took a recession in the early 1980s to purge the private sector of excessive inflationary expectations, and why many argued that wage and price controls would facilitate more rapid and less painful adjustment. Once the effect of unanticipated inflation is discounted, there remains the "natural rate" of unemployment or the "non-accelerating inflation rate of unemployment" (NAIRU). Changes in that "natural" rate have received much attention in recent years.[5] The basic relationship between the level of unemployment and real wage rates also implies that the "natural" rate of unemployment is positively related to the level of real wages. If wage rates are determined by collective bargaining, rather than by the competitive forces of supply and demand in the labour market, and the result is that wage rates are too high in the sense discussed above, then the "natural" rate of unemployment will be high.[6] If there is a public interest in the unemployment rate, then there is a public interest in the outcome of the system of collective bargaining.

All genuine unemployment has one basic characteristic. A person is unemployed because he cannot find employment at the current wage rate in a job he is competent to do. The only reason why he cannot find a job after reasonable search is because no employer would find it profitable to employ him. The only way he can be employed, other than by displacing another worker, is if the circumstances facing employers change so that it does become profitable to employ him.

At any prevailing set of product and factor prices, including the wage rate, a particular level of employment and the corresponding level of output will be most profitable for a particular firm. If that output cannot be sold at the current price, there is a problem of deficient demand. If prices are maintained, the quantity produced falls and fewer workers are employed. If the product price falls, the most profitable level of employment falls. The Keynesian remedy to this situation, when it arises throughout the economy, is to use monetary and fiscal policy to boost demand so that the equilibrium output can be sold. If that policy works, there is no longer a problem of deficient demand. But the firm still employs only the most profitable number of workers at current wages and prices. In aggregate, firms may not employ all the people who want to work. Firms will find it profitable to increase employment only if the product price rises relative to the wage rate, or the wage rate falls. If the real wage rate does not fall in an occupation with excess labour supply, persons excluded from the jobs they want and are qualified to do may seek employment in lower wage occupations. If there is an adequate non-union sector of the labour market where wage rates fall to accommodate them, they become underemployed. If there is not, there remains a problem of unemployment. In either case increased employment becomes profitable only at lower real wage rates. Thus even if monetary and fiscal policy worked perfectly to cure all problems of deficient demand at current prices, there would still be either unemployment or underemployment, or both, if real wage rates were too high. Only a fall in those real wage rates could alleviate that cause of the problem.

In the previous chapter it was argued that the system of collective bargaining may result in wage rates in some occupations that are inefficiently high. Qualified workers unable to find employment in those occupations may then find employment in lower wage occupations, in which case they are underemployed, or they may be unemployed. There is a legitimate public interest in having an efficient process of wage determination, without periodic disruption of production by strikes and lock-outs, and an efficient set of wage rates that achieve efficient utilization of labour. A system that results in excessive unemployment and underemployment clearly fails to satisfy the public interest in having an efficient labour market.

EQUITY

The basic reason for collective bargaining is that the indefinite period contract of employment leaves unspecified the wage rate at which employment will continue. The wage rate is agreed only for a definite period because it is impossible to predict far into the future all changes in relevant circumstances. When the wage rate is renegotiated, a dispute cannot be resolved by appeal to the criterion of integrity for there is no prior agreement. The costs of search, training, and mobility make a wide range of wage rates possible and it is necessary to apply the principles of equity in determining a fair wage rate for the ensuing period. The approach adopted by our society in the search for equity is contained in legislation that recognizes the respective rights of two parties, the employer and the union representing employees. Implicit in the approach is the belief that since one party will strive for a low wage rate and the other for a high wage rate, the outcome will depend on their respective bargaining power. If the legislation provides for an equitable balance of power between the parties, an equitable outcome should ensue. There are, however, three major problems with this approach.

The first problem is that the process is one of conflict, and conflict can be a very costly way to resolve a balance of power. Conflict works by each party inflicting damage, or threatening to inflict damage, on the other until they have yielded far enough to reach agreement. Damage is inflicted by temporary withdrawal from the contract of employment by strike or lockout, which interrupts the production process. Extensive damage may then be inflicted on third parties and there is no reason to expect the parties to the dispute to consider the costs to third parties when they embark on this means of conflict. The process is inefficient and the consequences for third parties inequitable. The public interest is violated on both grounds.

The second major problem is that the circumstances surrounding the negotiation process vary widely from case to case. It is in principle impossible to frame a single set of rules governing the negotiation process that will achieve equitable outcomes in all cases. The right to strike is a powerful weapon in the hands of a union that can inflict major damage on an employer in a short period to time. If the employer in question has the market power to reflect wage increases in product price increases, such a union may have the power to achieve high wage rates. That power is still greater if the damage inflicted on third parties results in effective pressure on the employer to yield. If the disruption to society is too great, however, legislation may be used to change the rules on an *ad hoc* basis, withdrawing the right to strike and requiring compulsory arbitration. A union that could not cause major damage even by a prolonged strike derives little power from the right to strike. Whatever the provisions of the law that defines the conditions surrounding the right to strike, those conditions may give too much power to some unions, too little to others, and illusory power to those with such great power to inflict damage that their rights would be withdrawn if exercised. No single set of rules could provide for a balance of power likely to lead to equitable outcomes in all cases.

The third problem is that specification of the respective rights of the two parties to the dispute ignores the interests of all other parties, although the principles of equity require that they too be treated fairly. The union may represent all those with an interest in securing high wages, but the employer does not represent all those with an interest in low wages. With lower real wage rates it would be profitable to employ more workers, to produce more output and reduce the product price in order to sell it, and to invest in capital complementary to labour. Potential workers qualified for the occupation in question but unable to secure employment in it are consigned to underemployment or unemployment. They have an interest in a lower wage rate that would increase employment. They are inequitably treated by comparison with workers currently in the occupation, but their interests are not represented in the process of collective bargaining. Workers who would remain in lower paid occupations would benefit if the supply of labour in their submarket were reduced as a consequence of increased employment in the occupation in question. But their interest in a lower wage rate is not represented. Potential customers who would buy the additional output that would result from greater employment in the occupation have an interest in a lower wage rate that would lead to increased output and reduced product price, but their interests are not represented. Investors who would provide the capital that would be needed to increase employment have an interest in a lower wage rate that would make expansion profitable, but they are not represented. The employer's interest in a lower wage rate coincides with that of all these parties, but he will not reckon the potential benefits to them when he decides when to yield to union pressure for a higher wage rate and when to bear the cost to him of prolonged conflict.[7]

The apparent faith of our society that stipulation of fair rules for the conflict process of collective bargaining will result in a fair outcome appears to be misplaced. There is no reason to suppose that the pattern of wage rates resulting from collective bargaining will be equitable in any sense. There is indeed strong evidence to suggest that the outcome is inequitable.

Workers in different occupations achieve wage rates that reflect their relative bargaining power, but relative bargaining power is not related to the relative values of their contributions to society nor to any other criterion of equity. The large numbers of qualified potential workers who are unable to secure employment in their chosen occupations clearly indicates inequity between those with such jobs and those denied the right to compete for them. Those in low wage occupations without powerful unions suffer the wage-depressing effects of excess competition for jobs there by those inequitably excluded from higher wage occupations. And the unemployed are inequitably excluded altogether from the labour market and consigned to survive frustrated on minimal support provided by taxpayers, who must inequitably bear that cost of the inefficiency of the labour market.

Defendants of the collective bargaining process, the power of unions, the right to strike, and the resultant wage rates also commonly base their arguments on grounds of equity. Their arguments have considerable historical validity and deserve respect. First they argue that in the absence of powerful unions, employers would have excessive power to exploit workers. In the last resort the only power a union has is the right to strike, and the outcome with unions with that power is more equitable then the outcome would be with unmatched power in the hands of employers. In the previous chapter I argued that a labour market in which the employer alone can set the wage rate results in inequitably low wage rates because the employer can expropriate the entire margin of rent afforded by mobility costs. In this chapter I have argued that the process of collective bargaining also results in serious inequities. There is little point in debating which of two inequitable systems is more inequitable, for I have no intention of recommending that we return to a system of unfettered employer power.

The second argument of the defendants of collective bargaining is more serious. The inequities identified as resulting from collective bargaining derive primarily from wage rates that are too high. Redressing those inequities would require reductions in those real wage rates and the consequence would be an increase in the return to capital or in profits. The only way to increase employment in particular occupations, or to attack a chronic unemployment problem in general, is to make it more attractive to employ workers. That is the essence of the argument that some real wage rates are inefficiently high. But on grounds of equity it could well be argued that the incomes of workers are not currently too high in relation to the incomes of those enjoying the returns to capital.[8] To reduce the former and increase the latter would then be inequitable. This argument can be made either with respect to a particular industry or with respect to the economy as a whole.

When an industry consists of only one or a few firms, the exercise of monopoly or oligopoly power in the product market may achieve abnormally high profits. If a powerful union succeeds in raising wage rates, those monopoly profits are shared with the workers. It could be argued that it is more equitable for the profits to be shared by capital and labour than for them to accrue entirely to capital. There is much merit to this argument when collective bargaining raises the wage rate from an initial monopsony position in which the wage rate is too low. A firm that has both monopoly power in the product market and monposony power in the labour market maximizes profit by restricting output to maintain a high product price and restricting employment to maintain a low wage rate. If a higher wage rate is enforced, by collective bargaining or other means, the employer can no longer depress the wage rate by restricting employment. Without that incentive to restrict employment, more workers are worth employing, more output is produced and the product price is reduced. When the wage rate is initially too low, raising it results in higher wages and more employment, more output and a lower product price, and lower monopoly profit.

The situation is quite different, however, if the wage rate is raised above the efficient level. The wage rate is too high when more qualified workers want jobs at the current wage than the firm finds it profitable to employ. Any increase in the wage rate then results in less employment, less output, and an increase in the product price. While a still higher wage rate reduces the monopoly profit of the firm, it does so at the expense of willing workers who are excluded, and customers who are either charged a higher price or priced out of the market.

High monopoly profits that accrue to capital, at the expense of consumers, may well be inequitable. There is much to be said for laws and regulations that control or limit the exercise of monopoly power. But raising a wage rate that is already too high only exacerbates the problem. When both the union and the firm exploit consumers and excluded workers, the extent of that exploitation is in total greater than when only the firm makes monopoly profit. Consideration of the appropriate policies to control the exercise of monopoly power in product markets lies outside the scope of this study. The conclusion as far as the labour market is concerned is clear, however. The extent of the problem of monopoly power is made worse by wage rates that are either too high or too low as judged by the criterion of efficiency. The wage rate is too high if more qualified workers want to work than the firm finds it profitable to employ.[9] A reduction in the wage rate would then serve the objective of equity as far as both consumers and excluded workers are concerned. It would also result in still higher monopoly profit for the firm, but that inequity would have to be addressed by other measures. The problem of monopoly profit for capital in a particular firm can only be made worse if workers in the firm also extract monopoly profit. It simply is not possible to mitigate the inefficiency and inequity that result from monopoly power in the product market by raising wage rates above, or depressing them below, the efficient level.

The argument that the return to capital throughout the economy is too high in relation to the return to labour, and that any reduction in wage rates would make the distribution between factors more inequitable, attempts to justify inefficiency on grounds of equity. The apparent conflict between efficiency and equity, however, is dependent on the assumption that two functions of the wage rate are necessarily inseparable. On the one hand, the wage rate is the price the employer must pay to employ labour and on the other, it is the income of the worker. In the discussion of efficiency I focused on the wage rate as the price of employing labour. In the discussion of equity I implicitly assumed that relative wage rates determined the relative incomes of different workers. But the actual income of a worker is his wage plus transfer payments less taxes. The ability to modify taxes and transfers makes it possible to separate the wage rate as the price of employing labour from the wage rate as the sole determinant of the worker's income.

We currently use a complex system of taxes, tax credits, and transfer payments to redistribute income. The system may well be unnecessarily complicated and there is much to be said in favour of consolidating many of our transfer payments into a single negative income tax system. Nevertheless, the potential for redistribution of income is by no means exhausted. Taxes and transfers can be geared to level of income and to individual circumstances or need, and they can be geared to source of income. If the use of efficient wage rates did result in higher returns to capital and lower returns to labour, it would be simple to compensate by imposing more of the tax burden on incomes derived from capital and less of the burden on incomes derived from labour. The distribution of income among owners of different factors is not necessarily tied to relative factor prices. Equity in the distribution of income is a question appropriately addressed by design of the tax system. My concern in this study is equity in the relative treatment of different members of the labour force. The inequities I have identified are inequities among workers in different occupations or between those employed and those denied access to the labour market. Such inequities are best addressed by appropriate pricing of labour as a factor of production.

In a market system the wage rate is the basic source of income for the worker, though for any given wage his income can be adjusted by taxes and transfers. The wage rate is similarly the basic statement of the cost of employing labour, though it too can be adjusted by taxation or subsidy of employers. In a system without fiscal intervention, the wage is both the total income of the worker and the total price of employing labour. With fiscal intervention it is neither. We are therefore free to use the wage rate itself in a number of different ways. In particular we can focus on the wage rate as the income of the worker or as the price of employing labour.

Our current practice is to focus on the wage rate as the worker's income. In order to achieve high workers' incomes we have designed a labour market based on collective bargaining that achieves high wage rates. The outcome, however, is not uniform and workers in some occupations have been able to use the power of collective bargaining to greater advantage than others. The resulting wage differences among occupations are not equitable, nor do they result in an efficient allocation of labour. The most obvious problem is that a significant proportion of the labour force is excluded from the labour market and consigned to unemployment. In effect we have used wages to provide incomes for most of the labour force and transfer payments to provide incomes for the rest. In the process we waste a significant proportion of our labour resources.[10]

We continue to insist that if a person is to be employed, his wage must provide an adequate basic income. Collective bargaining is used to achieve inefficiently high wages in some occupations, while a minimum wage for all occupations is enforced by law. We then approach the unemployment problem by a host of *ad hoc* schemes that either create jobs at the taxpayers' expense or subsidize employers to employ more workers at current wage rates. It may well be better to subsidize employment than to subsidize unemployment, but such a system fails to achieve either full or efficient use of our labour resources.

The alternative approach that is clearly indicated by the analysis in this study is to focus on the wage rate as the cost of employing labour. Efficient wage rates are those that result in the full utilization of the labour force and its optimal allocation among occupations. But efficient wages do not necessarily achieve equitable incomes for workers. Workers in different occupations would be equitably ranked and those with higher wage rates would properly enjoy higher incomes, for wage rates would reflect the value to society of the services performed and would constitute the incentive for workers to perform more valuable rather than less valuable roles in society. But the differences among wage rates may be inequitably great and those with the lowest wage rates may derive from their wages incomes that are intolerably low. Our value judgments may also suggest that the share of national income going to labour is too small in relation to that going to capital. We can then use taxes and transfers to address these problems of equity, imposing an appropriate tax burden on incomes from capital and on the higher labour incomes with negative taxes or transfer payments for those with the lower wage rates.

All three approaches rely on transfer payments to achieve equity. There is no way in which the labour market can achieve a structure of wage rates that alone will result in an equitable distribution of income. The first system transfers income to those excluded from the labour market, the second transfers it to selected employers, and the third to workers with the lowest wage incomes. Any of these three systems could in principle achieve an equitable distribution of total income, though the first would not achieve equity in the right of access to the labour market and the second could not achieve an efficient allocation of labour. The major advantages of the third system are that it achieves full and efficient use of our labour resources so that we have more national income in total to distribute, and it ranks workers in different occupations equitably in accordance with the value of their contributions to the economy, rather than inequitably in accordance with their power to threaten to disrupt the economy.

INTEGRITY

Society consists of a set of interdependence relationships among its members. Economic activity depends on the rights and responsibilities of individuals with respect to each other and to the system as a whole. Integrity is the respecting of rights and the honouring of responsibilities. Clearly there is a public interest in integrity for without it the system is jeopardized.

The essence of a market system is voluntary agreement to participate in acts of exchange. Such agreements are contracts and the law of contract is concerned with the enforcement of agreements. Not all agreements, however, are specified in such formal terms that they are enforceable in the courts. Whenever there is a promise to act in an certain way, or a clearly understood commitment, integrity requires that the promise or commitment be honoured. The indefinite period contract of employment is such a commitment to a continuing economic process that neither party will terminate without due notice. Continuous transactions in factor markets and product markets similarly generate the common understanding that goods and services will continue to be provided and purchased. Yet when the collective bargaining process results in a work stoppage by reason of strike or lock-out, the regular flows of goods and services are interrupted in related markets as well as the market in question. Suppliers and customers are suddenly denied the markets on which they have come to rely and the implicit commitment of continued availability is violated. This is a violation of the public interest in the integrity of the continuity of economic activity.

As important as the law of contract is the law of tort, which protects individuals from the damaging acts of others. Just as integrity requires that contracts be honoured so does it require that torts be not perpetrated. Yet on occasion strike action is threatened or taken with the clear expectation or even intention that it will cause severe loss, hardship, or inconvenience for innocent third parties. The public interest in integrity is violated.

Implicit in a market society is a social contract that entitles individuals to access to the markets on which they depend. Denial of such access is a violation of the implicit commitment by society to the individual. Clearly there is a public interest in such a breach of integrity. Yet the outcome of the collective bargaining process may well be to secure attractive wage rates for some while denying others the right to compete effectively in the labour market. The implicit denial of the right of access to markets, both for the unemployed and for the frustrated potential customers for the goods and services that the unemployed could produce, is a major breach of integrity with respect to the implicit social contract underlying a market society.

The system of collective bargaining, with final resolution of disputes by the conflict phase of strike or lock-out, fails to satisfy the public interest in efficiency, equity, and integrity. Yet it replaced a system in which employers had the power to specify wage rates that employees could individually only accept or reject. That system too failed to satisfy the three criteria. If we are to satisfy these criteria to a greater extent we must devise a different system. Before that challenge is addressed, however, we should inquire into the special features that characterize employment in the public sector and distinguish it from employment in the private sector of the economy. The public sector is the subject of the next chapter.

CHAPTER SIX

The Public Sector

The public sector can be defined in many different ways. A broad definition will be most appropriate for our purposes, though it will encompass many cases of employment that do not differ in significant ways from employment in the private sector. The public sector can be defined as activities that produce goods and services that are provided to citizens by government, or under the auspices of government, or by an agency of government that is publicly owned or funded to a significant extent by public money, or by a firm that is regulated by an agency of government. The important distinctions for my purposes between the public and private sectors are that in the public sector managerial decisions are made by elected politicians, or by persons directly or indirectly appointed by or responsible to elected politicians, and the goods and services produced are provided either without direct charge to the consumer or at prices intended to achieve a financial objective set directly or indirectly by government. The role of government is to replace the profit motive governing the private sector with other objectives intended to serve the public interest.

The public sector encompasses a wide range of diverse cases. At the centre are the operations of government itself, which include employment in all government departments at federal, provincial, and municipal levels. Included in this group are all those employed in the provision of public goods such as the judicial system, police and fire fighting services, and the construction and maintenance of streets and highways. Closely related are those employed in natural monopolies or public utilities owned and operated by government such as the post office, urban transit systems, and water and sewage systems.

The only distinction between public goods and public utilities is that in the former case pricing is not feasible and activities are funded by taxation, whereas in the latter case it is possible to charge consumers a price for services rendered. When prices can be charged, the activity could be profitable and it is not necessary that government operate it. Natural monopolies could be so profitable that when not operated by government they are often regulated by government. There is no important difference for my purposes between government ownership and government regulation. In both cases the financial objectives are set and prices are determined by government or agencies of government. Thus the fact that in Ontario electricity is produced by an organization owned by government, while natural gas is supplied by a regulated company, is a difference of no importance. Regulated companies must accordingly be considered part of the public sector. The last case is the provision of some services that are neither public goods nor natural monopolies, but are provided by government because the public interest requires that they be made available in greater quantities than they would be in a free market. The most important examples are education and health care, but this group also includes a wide range of other services such as municipal libraries and subsidized cultural activities.

The first important difference between the labour markets in the public and private sectors is that in the public sector the demand for the services of employees is determined through the political process, whereas in the private sector it is determined through the market process. A firm's demand for labour reflects the willingness of customers to pay for the product, though as we have seen above that reflection will be perfect only in the case of perfect competition. In the public sector, however, the demand of labour will reflect the number of workers that government, acting as the representative of citizens, considers it appropriate in the public interest to employ at various wage rates. Since government is not directly answerable to voters for every decision it makes, and decisions concerning employment in the public sector are often made by persons many stages removed from the politicians to whom they are ultimately responsible, there is no assurance that the demand for labour in the public sector will reflect perfectly the willingness of citizens to pay for services. The comparison between the demand for labour in the two sectors is between the imperfect reflection of customers' willingness to pay for the service and the imperfect reflection of citizens' willingness to pay for the service.

In the private sector the single firm may employ many workers of a particular type and accordingly has the power to decide the wage rate at which it will offer to employ them. It was argued above that the private employer has an incentive to exploit committed workers, offering inefficiently and inequitably low wages to expropriate the entire margin of rent afforded by the costs of search and mobility. The incentive in this case is the direct incentive of profit. Given the conditions of imperfect competition that make such exploitation possible, there is no reason to suppose that low wages will be reflected in low prices. The firm may thus fail fully to reflect customers' willingness to pay for the services of workers. The employing agency in the public sector has similar power, but is not motivated by profit. The incentive for the decision maker in the public sector, directly or indirectly, is the goodwill of voters. If committed workers are exploited by low wage offers, the expropriated rent accrues to taxpayers. There is no reason to suppose that voters as a whole are more possessed of the virtues of equity and integrity than entrepreneurs. When committed workers are exploited by low wage offers in the private sector, it is in the interest of profit, not as a reflection of customers' willingness to pay. When they are exploited in the public sector, it is in the interest of reflecting the desire of voters to reduce taxes or prices at the expense of their workers. In both cases the power of the employer to set the wage rate, with no countervailing power, can be expected to result in wage rates that are too low, violating the principles of equity and integrity with respect to committed workers, and violating efficiency as a consequence.

The power to exploit committed workers may be much greater in the public sector than in the private sector because that power derives from the immobility of workers, which may be greater in the public sector. When government has a monopoly in the provision of a good or service, whether because it is a natural monopoly or because legislation prohibits competition by the private sector, government is both the only supplier of the product and the only employer of workers with skills unique to that industry. If all medical services, education services, or nuclear reactors are in the public sector, then only government employs workers with the relevant skills. Since there is no scope for alternative employment of the human capital in question, the entire rent accruing to that capital could be expropriated by government if it had total power to set the relevant wage rates. In the absence of conscription, government faces the same necessity as other employers to offer wages and conditions of employment sufficiently attractive to entice new entrants to the occupation in question. But once a worker has committed himself to acquisition of the necessary skills, he has committed himself to work in the public sector if he is to derive a return from those skills. The magnitude of that return is not thereafter governed by market forces but is at the sole discretion of the employer.

The power to exploit workers is dependent on their immobility. Many employees in government monopolies possess skills that are not industry specific. They could readily find similar employment in the private sector and the scope for exploitation is then restricted to the same search and mobility costs that characterize employment in the private sector. Thus public sector hospitals have more power to exploit surgeons than to exploit janitors, and universities have more power to exploit professors then to exploit secretaries.[1]

In the private sector it was the power of employers to exploit committed workers that gave rise to the formation of unions and the practice of collective bargaining. Comparable or greater power in the public sector similarly encourages collusive behaviour by workers and collective bargaining characterizes the public sector too.[2] The power of a union to raise wages relies in the last resort on the power to strike. In the public sector that power may be either stronger or weaker than in the private sector. In the case of urgent and vital services a short strike may suffice to inflict such damage on the public that political pressure forces the employer to yield. A union with power to interrupt police service, fire protection service, health care services, or mail service has much greater power than is typical in the private sector. But when the service is not urgent, the power of the employer to survive a long strike depends on its resources. When a firm is closed by a strike, production and revenues stop while many costs continue. Eventually the firm may be forced to yield to avoid bankruptcy. But government does not face the prospect of bankruptcy. When services are provided to the public without direct charge, the source of revenue is taxation, and taxes continue during strikes. If the service is not urgent, however important it may be, the employer is in a stronger position to withstand a strike than firms in the private sector. Thus, for example, if the gardeners in municipal parks called a strike, it would be possible to permit the grass and weeds to grow for a long time without great political pressure from the public to yield.

The right to strike is a right granted by law. Government is the source of law. The great power of some public sector unions to inflict damage and inconvenience on society by strike action may be nullified at any time by legislative action. Government is both one party to the collective bargaining process in the public sector and the framer of the rules of the game. The right to strike may be suspended on an *ad hoc* basis, or the outcome may be stipulated by guidelines or wage controls that override the collective bargaining process.[3] Unions in the public sector may be very weak or very strong. The strike threat may be of no avail or a weapon of great power. In cases where the strike is most powerful, however, the right to strike may be withdrawn and the union rendered impotent. There is no reason to suppose that such a diverse range of cases can be encompassed by a single process or set of rules that will achieve outcomes that accord with the principles of efficiency, equity, or integrity.

In the private sector we found that no single set of rules governing the process of collective bargaining, strikes, and lockouts could ensure an appropriate balance of power between employers and employees in all cases. In some cases employers retain the power to exploit workers despite the existence of unions and the right to strike. In others, unions have sufficient power to achieve for their members wage rates that are above the efficient level. Some wage rates are inefficiently high, some inefficiently low, and the criteria of equity and integrity are violated both with respect to the relative wage rates of different groups of workers and with respect to society as a whole. The same holds true in the public sector, but the nature of the public sector, characterized as it is by government monopoly of the provision of essential services, is such that the power of both employer and employees is greater than in the private sector. The potential for undue exploitation of committed workers is greater in the public sector because workers with specialized skills have no alternative employment. The potential for undue exploitation of society by a powerful union is also greater because government monopoly means that citizens have no substitute source of supply. The problems of collective bargaining that arise in the private sector arise in more extreme form in the public sector, which is why the right to strike is more commonly denied or withdrawn in the public sector than it is in the private sector.

Efficiency in the use of our labour resources is as important in the public sector as it is in the private sector. But efficiency will not be achieved if public sector wage rates are either too low or too high. If wage rates are too low for new entrants to the occupation, there will be inadequate incentive to attract good applicants. If they are too low for already established and committed employees, the workers become demoralized and new recruits foresee poor prospects for themselves. In either event the public sector will encounter difficulty in competing with the private sector for the most highly qualified and ambitious entrants to the occupation. When public sector employers offer wage rates lower than citizens would be willing to pay to have the service performed, and performed well, workers prefer to enter private sector employment even though their services would be more valuable to society in the public sector. The consequence is a misallocation of labour.

When wage rates in the public sector are too high, society economizes excessively in the employment of workers. High wage rates must be reflected in either high prices or high taxes. Political pressure then persuades the employing agency to restrict the number of workers. The quantity and quality of service to the public are both affected adversely. Economy in the use of scarce resources is desirable, but excessive economy results when the scarcity is exaggerated by wage rates that are too high. Public services are poorly provided and facilities are inadequate because the cost of the necessary workers is perceived to be high, while the labour of the potential additional workers is wasted in unemployment. The cost to society of employing workers who would otherwise be unemployed is in fact very low, but a high wage rate makes it appear high to each separate public sector employing agency. Each agency endeavours to balance its own budget with politically acceptable prices or tax rates, while a different level or department of government appears responsible for the unemployed. Taxpayers who are reluctant to employ more workers at high wage rates face instead the high tax burden of supporting the unemployed. Some potential workers are fortunate and secure well-paid employment in the public sector, while others are unemployed and survive on much less. The taxpayer pays both, but inefficiently high wage rates result in his receiving no services from the unemployed.

When wage rates are too high there is incentive to invest excessively in labour-saving capital. The public sector then competes with the private sector for capital because capital appears cheaper than the labour it replaces. The cost of capital may well be lower than the cost of labour at the prevailing wage rate in the public sector, while being higher than the opportunity cost of using that labour. The taxpayer then pays for the capital more than he would have to pay for labour at an efficient wage rate, and must also support the potential workers in unemployment. Capital is inefficiently allocated and labour wasted.

Many industries in the public sector are publicly owned or publicly regulated because they are natural monopolies. If they were privately owned and unregulated they could yield high monopoly profits. Under conditions of monopoly, profit is maximized by charging a price higher than production cost and reducing the volume of output to sustain the high price. Quite apart from the issue of equity involved in such exploitation of the consumer is the inefficient allocation of resources. The common solution to this problem is to regulate price and guarantee service to all consumers willing to pay the regulated price. But price is not regulated at an efficient level, it is regulated at a level that will cover costs and yield a fair return to capital. The consumer or taxpayer is charged a price or tax that covers the cost of capital and the wage cost of labour. Monopoly profits do not arise. But if a powerful union is able to achieve wage rates that are inefficiently high, those wages will be reflected in prices. It is precisely in the essential public utilities and public services that unions have greatest power, because even a short strike can cause severe costs. Thus there arises the paradoxical result that public ownership or regulation is used to prevent the owners of capital from exploiting the public by setting prices that yield monopoly profit, while permitting a powerful union to set wage rates that yield monopoly rents. The problems of inefficiency and inequity that result from monopoly power are the same whether monopoly power is wielded by the owners of capital of the owners of labour. We regulate prices in the public interest, but set prices that reflect wage rates that result from the collective bargaining process. If those wage rates are inefficiently high, they are not in the public interest and the inefficient consequence of monopoly power is still suffered.

The criterion of equity refers to fairness in the relative treatment of different people. The very nature of the process by which wage rates are determined in the public sector must lead us to expect that it will result in inequities among different groups of public sector employees. The power of the public sector employer to pay inequitably low wage rates is greatest in the case of workers with skills specific to public sector employment. It is weakest in the case of workers who are mobile between public and private sector employment. The power of employees to achieve inequitably high wages is greatest in public sector monopolies providing vital and urgent services for which there is no substitute. It is weakest when the service, however important, is not urgent. Since there is no reason to suppose that the circumstances giving rise to strong or weak employer power will coincide with those giving rise to comparable employee power, we must expect individual cases to vary widely in the balance of bargaining strength. As a consequence we must expect that some wage rates will be inequitably high and some inequitably low.

As the earlier discussion demonstrated, inequities also exist among different submarkets of the labour market in the private sector. It is then inevitable that inequities must prevail between the private and public sectors. Inequitably high wage rates in the public sector will be high in relation to inequitably low wage rates in the private sector, and inequitably low wage rates in the public sector will be low in relation to inequitably high wage rates in the private sector. It is more difficult to assess whether wage rates in the public sector as a whole are inequitable in relation to private sector wage rates as a whole.[4]

Government policies that affect public sector wage rates can be used in an attempt either to follow or to lead the private sector, and either policy can result in inequities. Those responsible for setting wage rates in the public sector, whether they are set by the employer or by arbitration, may seek to achieve equitable comparability with similar wage rates in the private sector. When similar occupations exist in both sectors, and workers are freely mobile between sectors, the public and private sectors are both parts of the same labour market. An attempt by one part to follow the other is no more than an assessment of market forces by which both are bound.

Where comparable occupations do not exist in both sectors, however, comparison is more difficult. Highly skilled workers are often highly specialized and their skills may be specific to a particular occupation or sector. It may not be possible to compare the wage rate of a particular group of public sector employees with that of comparable workers in the private sector, for there may be no comparable workers in the private sector. All that can then be attempted is a comparison with comparably skilled private sector employees whose skills may be quite different. Years and cost of necessary training may be one basis of comparison. Specialized workers are, however, immobile among submarkets in the private sector and chapter 3 showed how changing demand patterns could result in substantial and inequitable differences among wage rates in different submarkets when workers are immobile among them. The outcome of collective bargaining may also vary widely among different private sector submarkets. Thus it may be possible to find different occupations in the private sector in which wage rates vary widely although all satisfy some simple criterion, such as years of training, of comparability with the public sector group in question. It is then clearly impossible to establish for the public sector group a wage rate equitably comparable with all relevant private sector groups. The best that the wage setter or arbitrator could do would be to seek some form of average of comparable private sector wage rates. There is, of course, no assurance that any average in the private sector reflects equity with respect to the rest of society.

When government policy is used to set public sector wage rates in an attempt to lead the private sector by example, it may be intended either to improve or restrain wage rates and other conditions of employment. Citizens expect government to behave in an ethical and equitable manner. Voters hold governments accountable for their actions. The public sector is typically the first to abolish discrimination on grounds of sex or race to set an example for private sector employers. Public sympathy is always greatest for the poorest members of society.[5] Government, in the interest of vertical equity, may well pay its lowest paid workers more than private sector employers of similar workers. If example does not suffice, private sector employers may be forced to comply by minimum wage legislation. The problem with this approach is that the search for equitable incomes may be in conflict with the need for efficient wage rates. Even though the minimum wage may result in extensive unemployment among young, unskilled, and inexperienced workers, a government may claim credit for ensuring that the lowest paid workers receive a decent living wage. Each sector may then blame the other for not creating more such employment.

When high wage rates are perceived to be a widespread problem, and when the rate of increase in wage rates is perceived to be inflationary, government may wish to set an example for the private sector by restraining wages. Public sympathy will again be greatest for the lowest paid workers, and guidelines or controls may be applied with greatest severity on highly paid workers. When government attempts to set examples both of paying low wage workers more and of paying high wage workers less, the inevitable consequence is that wage differentials in the public sector tend to be narrower than in the private sector. Thus the wage rates of highly skilled workers paid the highest wages in the public sector may be inequitably low by comparison with the private sector, while the wage rates of the lowest paid occupations in the public sector are inequitably high. Clearly vertical equity cannot then be achieved in both sectors.

The criterion of equity between public sector employees and society as a whole must also be considered. In the discussion of efficiency I considered the potential for powerful unions in public sector monopolies to exploit customers and citizens by extracting monopoly rents that result in high prices or taxes.[6] Such monopoly rents are inefficient and the exploitation of society by a group with such monopoly power is also inequitable. When wage rates are inefficiently high, the level of employment is inefficiently low. Monopoly wage rates can be maintained only if other potential workers are prevented from competing for jobs. The ability to exclude competing workers is one characteristic power of a union in the collective bargaining process. The inequity inflicted on the unemployed and the underemployed by unions that maintain inefficiently and inequitably high wage rates for those already employed was discussed in the consideration of collective bargaining in the private sector. As we have seen, however, the characteristics of the public sector are such that it is most likely to achieve inefficiently high wage rates in low wage occupations, while the power of government to exploit its workers is greatest in highly skilled and specialized occupations. When unemployment is focused on young, unskilled, and inexperienced workers, who are potential candidates for low wage occupations, the inequity is between those with jobs in low wage occupations and those without jobs. The process of wage setting in the public sector may then be a more serious source of such inequity than that in the private sector.

The wage rates that prevail in occupations for which large numbers of unemployed potential workers are qualified do not always result from deliberate attempts by government to achieve higher wages in low wage occupations. Government is responsible for the minimum wage law, but many unemployed potential workers possess skills comparable with those employed at wage rates considerably in excess of the statutory minimum. In such cases the inequity between the employed and the unemployed results from the process of collective bargaining in both the public and private sectors. Only where the monopoly power of the public sector union results in its achieving wage rates that are inequitably high by comparison with comparable workers in the private sector can we consider collective bargaining in the public sector to be a more serious source of the problem than collective bargaining in the private sector.

The criterion of integrity is particularly important in the public sector because the specific skills of some public sector employees preclude their mobility. The acquisition of human capital is an expensive investment. A person who acquires the necessary skill and experience to serve society in the public sector, with little prospect of deriving an adequate return from those skills in private sector employment, does so in the expectation that he will be employed in the public sector. Such persons are committed to the public sector. Since the relevant employing agency in the public sector is a monopoly, the individual worker is tied to a particular employer. If we are to have an efficient allocation of resources to investment in such human capital, the individual must be protected from the risk inherent in acquiring specialized skills that render him highly immobile.

This reason for job security is quite distinct from the reasons for tenure in sensitive occupations. Members of the judicial and academic professions are granted tenure because it is vital to the proper performance of their role in society that they be free from any threat of victimization if their thoughts and actions are unpopular or embarrassing. Judicial independence and academic freedom both require protection of the individual whose job it is to be honest rather than tactful. Both the reasons for job security and the reasons for tenure make it appropriate that contracts of employment in public sector occupations requiring high levels of job specific skills be long term. When the individual acquires the skills necessary to serve society in such a role, he implicitly makes a long-term commitment to such service. If we are to have efficient incentive for such investment in human capital, that long-term commitment by the individual must be matched by comparable long-term commitment by society to the individual. Integrity requires that such commitment be honoured.

Chapter 3 argued that advance specification of remuneration in a long-term employment contract is extremely difficult. Changing economic conditions require that money wage rates be adjusted periodically in ways that can never fully be foreseen. This problem is greatest when the contract is implicitly for an entire career. Both parties are then committed to a contract, the terms of which are not specified. Collective bargaining provides a poor solution to this problem because both parties have enormous potential power and the range for bargaining is very wide. When workers are highly immobile, an unscrupulous employer can impose substantial reductions in real wage rates without fear of losing their services. When no qualified potential workers exist outside the contract in question, an unscrupulous union providing a vital service could secure substantial increases in real wage rates without fear of losing employment. The process of collective bargaining provides no assurance of a reasonable outcome and no protection from major breaches of integrity by either party.

The public sector uses the same process of collective bargaining as in the private sector. It suffers from the same limitations in both sectors when judged by the criteria of efficiency, equity, and integrity. But the circumstances of the public sector make those limitations more severe. When there are many competing employers, many competing employees, and perfect mobility, a competitive market works perfectly. It is precisely the absence of these conditions that gives rise to the central problems of the labour market and to the use of collective bargaining as an alternative process. In the private sector, when there are a number of employers of workers in a particular occupation, albeit not a large number, and each indulges in collective bargaining with a separate union, the potential bargaining range may be narrow. The process of conflict inherent in collective bargaining may violate our criteria of efficiency, equity, and integrity, but the scope for such violation is limited. The public sector, however, is characterized by monopoly. There is no other employer, society has no alternative source of supply of the goods and services in question, and those services are in many cases both vital and urgent. The potential bargaining range is then wide, the costs of conflict for third parties extreme, and the extent of the violation of the criteria of efficiency, equity, and integrity may be severe.

The process of collective bargaining has been shown to be very far from a perfect solution to the problem of determining wage rates in the labour market. It would be an acceptable solution, albeit an unsatisfactory one, only if no alternative system would satisfy the three criteria to a greater extent. In the next chapter, I shall endeavour to find a better alternative.

CHAPTER SEVEN

The Better Alternative

Previous chapters have examined the working of various possible forms of the labour market ranging from the perfectly competitive spot market that satisfies the assumptions of the simple model of supply and demand to the system of collective bargaining that characterizes the contemporary real world. Each has been assessed by the three criteria of efficiency, equity, and integrity. The general conclusion is that the unavoidable existence of high costs of search, training, and mobility preclude the achievement of sufficient flexibility in the labour market for a system based on supply and demand alone to work satisfactorily. The essential characteristic that makes the free market optimal is the absence of power in the hands of any party to influence the price, or wage rate, at which the services of labour are bought and sold. Modern technology requires large-scale firms and with size in the market there inevitably goes power to influence price. In the public sector power derives from the monopoly inherent in government. With immobility there cannot be perfect competition, which relies on sellers being freely and costlessly able to sell to alternative buyers, and buyers being similarly free to buy from alternative sellers. Power and immobility together provide scope for exploitation.

The system of collective bargaining recognizes the inevitable existence of power and endeavours to balance it on the two sides of the market. But balanced power is a very different thing from the absence of power. In the absence of power we have competition, with balanced power we have conflict. Whatever the rules prescribed for the exercise of power in a context of conflict, both the process and the outcome fail to satisfy the criteria of efficiency, equity, and integrity. The complex interdependence relationships of the modern economy result in many people other than the immediate participants having a vital interest in the process by which each employment contract is negotiated and the outcome achieved. There is a strong and legitimate public interest in the functioning of the labour market. That interest is seriously violated by a system of collective bargaining that relies on the conflict phase of strike or lock-out to resolve disputes.

Dissatisfaction with the current system requires a search for a better way. That search is not an attempt to design a new society. Revolution is neither desirable nor feasible, for there is too much good in the current set of principles and institutions to risk jeopardizing the good in a vain search for the best. Our society is deeply attached to the principles of freedom that underlie our economic system, and for good reason. History unfolds best by evolution not revolution, and the basic fabric of our society must be retained. But improvement is always possible. It can be achieved only by change and the smooth evolution of society is a continuous process of change. Thus the challenge is to retain all that is good in our current social system while effecting a solution to the identified problems. In devising a solution, we must be bound by the principle of minimum necessary change. The following principles must be retained and if possible enhanced.

THE PRINCIPLES

The first and most important principle is individual freedom. We must never forget that the unit of human labour is a human being, that the system exists to serve the interest of human beings, and that individuals are the best judges of their own interests. No system can provide freedom from economic scarcity. To consume we must produce, and to produce we must work. But the economic constraints of available resources and known technology leave wide scope for choice of what to produce, how to produce, and how much to produce. Individual freedom means that each individual is free to choose his role in society, and to enjoy rewards commensurate with the value of his service to society. Each human being is a self-proprietor of his own human capital and should be free to decide the nature and extent of its employment, constrained only by the range of possibilities that exist for him to play a valuable role in the social and economic structure. The function of the labour market is to present the individual with a range of options that validly reflect the economic possibilities.

The institution of private property means that within the private sector land and capital are privately owned. Individual freedom means that the owner of land or physical capital, like the self-proprietor of human capital, is free to decide on the extent to which and the way in which his resources will be employed in the service of society. It is the function of markets to present individuals with options and incentives that validly reflect the values to society of the various possibilities.

The way in which markets present individuals with options is by providing opportunities to enter into contracts. A contract is a voluntary exchange of obligations. Individual freedom means that no individual should be bound by a contract unless he has voluntarily entered into it. The decision to enter a particular contract is voluntary only if the individual has available to him a range of alternatives that validly represent the economic constraints governing society as a whole. If the conditions of the options open to him fully reflect both the value of the service to society entailed in each option and any costs or adverse effects that each option would impose on others, it also follows that any contract that is made voluntarily by both parties is legitimate. Freedom means both freedom to enter contracts and freedom to refuse to do so.

Freedom to enter contracts implies freedom to negotiate contracts, to bargain over their terms, and to associate with others in the bargaining process. The option of collective bargaining should be constrained by the same principles that should bind all options, namely that the individual or individuals involved should face conditions that reflect both the benefits and the costs that would result for the economic system. Limits to collective bargaining arise only when collusion results in the power to exploit others. Freedom of contract and freedom of association do not imply freedom to conspire to inflict harm on others or deny others access to markets with comparable freedom to negotiate contracts.

The second principle, integrity, is vital to an economic system based on free contract. Freedom of contract is meaningful only if there is confident expectation that contracts will be honoured. Just as no individual should be bound by a contract that he has not freely entered, so should all individuals be bound by the terms of contracts they have voluntarily made. The enforcement of contracts, and the interpretation of contracts in cases of ambiguity, requires a legal system to which any individual may appeal to have disputes arising from contracts fairly adjudicated. Constraints on freedom are justified only in the cause of protecting the freedom of others. Individual freedom is protected by the rule of law. The principle of integrity requires the existence of a legal system capable of protecting individual freedom. The law of contract serves to enforce the terms of contracts voluntarily made and the law of tort to protect individuals whose freedom is violated by the actions of others. Criminal law exists to protect society from acts by individuals that are detrimental to society as a whole.

The third principle, equity, was discussed in chapter 2. It requires that individuals have equal rights as members of the economic society and in particular that they have equal right of access to markets in which they can voluntarily enter into contracts with terms reflecting the values to society of the services they contract to perform or the goods and services they acquire. Equity requires that disputes between individuals be resolved fairly and in particular that the paradox resulting from effective commitment to an indefinite period contract of employment, without contractual specification of the conditions of employment or amount of remuneration, be resolved fairly. Equity requires that the relative wage rates attaching to different occupations reflect the relative values of those occupations to society. This aspect of equity will be achieved, at least in the private sector, if the principles of freedom of contract and freedom of access to markets outlined above are satisfied.

Equity also requires fairness in the distribution of income. It is fair that persons who perform services of greater value to society should receive greater incomes than those whose service are of lesser value, but it is not necessarily fair that income should be strictly proportional to the value of services performed. This is particularly important for persons who are unable to perform services of significant value. Children, the elderly, and the infirm may perform no current services, yet a compassionate society ensures that they receive at least minimum sustenance by the transfer of income from those currently performing valuable services. It is the function of our tax and transfer system to redistribute income. Society must decide through the political process the extent to which low wage earners should have their incomes supplemented and high wage earners their incomes reduced. Appropriate mechanisms for such transfers already exist or can readily be devised. They are not the principal concern of this study. Its concern is to ensure that whatever distribution of disposable income is to be achieved by taxes and transfers, pre-tax wage rates should reflect the value of services. This is vital because those pre-tax wage rates serve both as the incentives that guide individuals in their choice of occupation and as the prices that employers must pay to use a valuable resource. The proper pricing of labour services is necessary if a market system based on free contract is to function efficiently.

Efficiency is the fourth principle. Whatever the chosen distribution of disposable income, it is important that the goods and services that disposable income is used to buy are produced efficiently. In particular the services of the labour force should be used efficiently and this can be achieved only if those who employ such services are charged for them a price, or wage, that properly reflects their alternative value to society. The properties of an efficient labour market – full utilization, proper allocation, and efficient degrees of security and mobility – have been examined in previous chapters.

POSSIBLE FORMS OF THE LABOUR MARKET

There are only a limited number of ways in which a labour market can be organized that accord with our principles of individual freedom of contract and self-proprietorship of human capital. The three well-known forms have been analysed in previous chapters and a summary of the conclusions will suffice here.

Perfect competition is, of course, an optimal market form where appropriate conditions exist. Some parts of the labour market, notably the spot market and the market for casual labour, are characterized by conditions that permit the operation of perfect competition. But those conditions do not exist in much of the labour market and perfect competition there simply is not possible. Modern technology requires large-scale firms and when employers are both big and few, perfect competition among them is not possible. The public sector is characterized by monopoly, and monopoly of the product implies monopsony in the market for specialized labour. The high costs of search, training, and mobility for both employers and employees preclude the flexibility of employment that would be needed for perfect competition. Competitive forces cannot operate when strong ties exist between particular buyers and sellers, yet high mobility costs require continuing commitment of employers and employees to each other. For these reasons perfect competition cannot be the common form of the labour market, although it can exist in some submarkets without violating any of the principles.

When the conditions necessary for perfect competition break down, the labour market becomes monopsonistic, the single employer of many workers having the power to set the wage rate that individual employees can only accept or reject. Acceptance of employment by the individual worker does not constitute a voluntary contract as required by the principle of freedom when the individual does not have the right to negotiate and does not have available a range of options fairly reflecting the value of his services in all possible alternative occupations. Monopsony often exists in the absence of unions, was typical before unions were formed, and would exist again if the power of unions were severely curtailed. While growth in the total size of the labour market, greater urban population density, and increased geographical mobility of labour have tended to reduce the potential for monopsony power, increased specialization of labour and the larger efficient size of firms required by modern technology have tended to increase it. Monopsony may be a reasonably efficient form of the labour market, but is grossly inequitable. It is characterized by a captive labour force, a wide margin of rent between the highest wage that employers would pay and the lowest that workers would accept, and the power of employers to exploit workers by expropriating the entire rent margin. The principal reason why unions were formed and sanctioned by law was to balance and offset the inequitable power of the employer over individual employees and employees as a group. Certainly it is neither desirable nor politically feasible to restore unfettered monopsony power to the labour market.

The monopsony power of the employer is matched by the united power of employees in the system of collective bargaining. When that system works well it satisfies the necessary principles. When negotiations break down it does not. Clearly it would be advantageous to retain the benefits of the process while protecting society from its adverse consequences. The benefits are many. The parties are free to negotiate and voluntarily agree the terms of contracts. If the parties are reasonably matched in power, the strength of each affords protection from exploitation by the other. The continuing commitment of employers and employees to each other that is efficient in view of the high costs of search, training, and mobility can be achieved by the indefinite period contract, the terms of which can be revised periodically by agreement after negotiation. If agreement is genuinely voluntary, there is no violation of the principle of freedom of contract, the process is efficient, the outcome equitable, and the explicit statement of the terms and conditions of employment in a written contract facilitates its enforcement with integrity.

But the process of collective bargaining does not always work well. Agreement is not genuinely voluntary when coercion is used. When negotiation fails to achieve an outcome both parties are content to accept, each is confronted with only two options. It can accept the other party's offer or proceed to resolve the dispute by conflict. Conflict is inherently inefficient for the essence of the process is that each party endeavours to impose costs on the other in order to coerce it into agreement. If the parties are unevenly matched in their power to inflict damage, the weaker party may submit when confronted with the threat of conflict. When the employer is strong and the union weak, employees may be coerced into accepting a wage rate that is inefficiently and inequitably low. When the union in strong, and the employer is in a weak position to withstand a work stoppage, the employer may be coerced into accepting a wage rate that is inefficiently and inequitably high. A new contract may be agreed, but the principles are violated when agreement is achieved by coercion, for agreement is not genuinely voluntary when the only alternative is to suffer the costs of conflict with a stronger adversary.

When coercion by the threat of conflict results in a wage rate that is either too high or too low, the consequence is inefficiency. Labour is inefficiently allocated among firms and occupations, and capital is inefficiently allocated because the relative incentives to invest in labour-saving or employment-creating capital are distorted. When the wage rate is inefficiently high, too few workers will be employed. This diverts labour to other submarkets and depresses wage rates there. If the problem of excessively high wage rates is widespread, the consequence may be unemployment and the exclusion of many potential workers from access to the labour market. Equity within the society is violated as well as efficiency.

If the parties are evenly matched, or if each believes that it

is in the stronger position to withstand conflict, both may refuse to yield to coercion and the conflict phase ensues. The
labour market is the only case in our society in which the
law provides for resolution of disputes through the process of
trial by combat.[1] Production stops, causing loss to both parties and perhaps inflicting serious costs on suppliers, consumers, and the public at large. The process is both inefficient
and inequitable and there is no reason to suppose that the outcome satisfies any of the principles. Either party may be coerced
by conflict into agreeing to a wage rate that is either too high
or too low. The legitimate interests of one party and the public interest are both violated. The problems with conflict are
most acute in the public sector because of the monopoly nature of government and government-owned or regulated industries, but they are not unique to the public sector. In the
private sector the outcome may be anywhere in the bargaining range defined by the most employers would be willing to
pay and the least employees would be willing to accept. The
range of settlements, some too high and some too low, gives
rise to inefficiency in the allocation of labour and inequity
among workers in different occupations. Focus of the conflict
on the principal parties, with no mechanism to reflect the interests of specific third parties or the public at large, can result in failure to achieve full utilization of our labour resources
and exclusion of a significant proportion of the population from
the labour market. When potential workers and potential customers for their products are denied access to markets, they
are denied their basic right to freedom of contract. No one has
the right to a contract unless another party is willing to agree
to one. The denial of the right to contract arises when there
is collusive agreement to refuse to contract or when one party
is coerced into refusing to contract. A potential employer and
employee may be willing to agree to the terms of a contract,
but cannot do so if a collective agreement prescribes a higher
wage rate in the occupation in question. The employer and
the union have then collusively agreed to exclude the potential employee from the labour market. The employer may have
been coerced into the agreement by a strong union and com-
pelled to agree to refuse to enter lower wage employment contracts in order to secure the services of the large group of
union members. While the employer has been party to the decision that he will refuse to contract with the potential worker,
and has the right to refuse to contract, the potential em-

ployee was not party to the collective agreement that denies him the opportunity to compete for contracts of employment.

When the market system fails to achieve either a process or an outcome acceptable to society, the political process is commonly invoked to impose a solution. Wage and price controls have been used as temporary emergency expedients during periods of rapid inflation, but they typically specify only maximum rates of increase. In themselves they do nothing to redress imbalance in relative wages or prices. The problems that derive from imperfect markets, and particularly from monopoly and monopsony power in both product and labour markets, are the consequence of the simultaneous existence of different degrees of power in different markets. It is, of course, possible to have all wages and prices under state control with a system in which government, or some government agency, has discretionary control over each price and wage rate separately. But such a system implies a degree of state control of the economy that would be incompatible with the fundamental principles of a market economy.

In product markets a number of different policies are used to address specific problems. Antitrust or anticombines legislation prohibits the excessive and unnecessary concentration of power in product markets and the practice of collusion among firms that should compete. When monopoly is necessary on grounds of efficiency, the industry is either state owned or controlled by a regulatory agency. When an industry is characterized by what is perceived as excessive competition, controlled monopoly power is created by statute and vested in a marketing board. Disparities of market power are offset by discretionary use of tariffs or other controls on international trade to protect weak firms from foreign competition and subject strong ones to it. The armoury of weapons available to government to offset disparities of monopoly power in product markets may leave much to be desired and improvements are worth seeking, but that problem lies outside the scope of this study. The important conclusion of the discussion of the public interest in chapter 5 was that wage rate policy is not an appropriate tool to offset monopoly power in product markets. Wage rates above or below the efficient level exacerbate rather than ameliorate the problem of monopoly.

The problems of monopoly and monopsony power in labour markets are in principle similar to those in product markets, but the circumstances are different and different solutions have been used. Statutory limits on the rate of increase in wages may be useful as a temporary expedient in a period of rapid inflation, but the great disparities that exist among different submarkets could be addressed only by discretionary control. Selective and discretionary use of wage controls would imply total control of the labour market and correspondingly total control of the economy. Regulation of wage rates is not a satisfactory solution in our economy because it would be either too strong or too weak. Total regulation of absolute and relative wage rates, as well as rates of change in wage rates, would be too strong. It would amount to regulation of the entire labour market and would be incompatible with our principles of freedom. Yet control measures that stop short of total regulation would fail to address the basic problem.

Use of the principle of countervailing power through the process of collective bargaining has been the standard policy used to address the problem of power in labour markets, but both the process of conflict and the resulting set of wage rates fail to satisfy the objectives of efficiency, equity, and integrity. In product markets where monopoly is unavoidable, we create regulatory agencies to balance the interests of producers, consumers, and the public at large. Prices are set by what is essentially a process of arbitration among conflicting interests. In labour markets arbitration is used only for some essential public services and as an *ad hoc* expedient in other cases. We have chosen to use collective bargaining rather than arbitration as the standard system.

Collective bargaining is viable when it works well, but all too often the threat or exercise of coercion through conflict results in unacceptable outcomes. Perfect competition is impossible in much of the labour market, monopsony is unacceptably inequitable, and regulation is either too comprehensive or ineffective. The time has come to consider seriously the more extensive use of arbitration.

ARBITRATION

Arbitration is the settlement of a dispute by an independent party to whom the disputants have presented the facts and arguments. It differs from regulation because it cannot be used to override voluntary agreement. Thus the use of arbitration at the dispute phase of collective bargaining permits retention of the process of negotiation leading to voluntary agreement. Only when the parties cannot agree is the dispute phase reached. If conciliation and mediation fail to achieve agreement, the choice then is between resolution by conflict and resolution by arbitration.

The way in which a dispute would be resolved should the need arise has a significant effect on the process of negotiation. Agreement is reached when one party is willing to accept an offer made by the other. In the early stages of negotiation an offer by one party leaves the other with the choice of accepting it or making a counter offer. As the parties consecutively revise their previous offers, the range of disagreement narrows until one party accepts the other's offer and agreement is reached. At any stage either party may refuse to revise its previous offer. If both refuse to revise their offers further, each has the choice of accepting the other's offer, in which case there is agreement, or of proceeding to a dispute. The willingness of each party either to revise its own offer or accept the other's offer clearly depends on its anticipation of the outcome of a dispute.

If a dispute would be resolved by the conflict phase of strike or lock-out, each party must assess its prospects of coercing the other into submission. If one party is clearly in a stronger position than the other to withstand a work stoppage, the strong party may stop the process of offer revision early and confront the other with the option of accepting an unreasonable offer or being coerced into submission. If, however, a dispute would be resolved by arbitration, each must assess what the outcome of arbitration would be.[2] A strong party, confident of its ability to outlast the other in a work stoppage, may be much less sanguine about its prospects of persuading an arbitrator that its current offer is reasonable. A strong party may coerce an adversary but not an arbitrator. Faced with the prospect of arbitration, the strong party will be willing to revise its offer further and the prospects of agreement being reached without dispute are enhanced.

Our principle of freedom requires that contracts be genuinely voluntary. Agreement to a contract is voluntary only when each party has a reasonable alternative. The case for arbitration rests on its being a more reasonable alternative than conflict. The alternative of conflict may be an acceptable alternative to a strong party, but not to a weak one. It may be the only alternative if society provides no other. In a lawless frontier society the alternative to agreement between neighbours may be recourse to battle. In such a society the right to bear arms may appear precious. But only the bully laments the development of a system of law and order. In the labour market the only alternative to accepting the other's offer is conflict, and the right to strike is preciously defended. But it too could become obsolete if a just process of dispute arbitration is developed.

Conflict is a very costly process for the two parties. When there is a work stoppage both parties suffer losses, perhaps for a long period of time. Arbitration is not free, but the costs of arbitration are much lower than the costs of conflict. A party that would be in a weak position in the event of conflict will be much more willing to hold out for a reasonable contract at the risk of facing arbitration than it would at the risk of facing conflict. When the alternative to agreement is arbitration, agreement will be more genuinely voluntary than when the alternative is conflict. Thus the first advantage of arbitration over conflict arises in negotiations that would not reach the stage of dispute in either event. The option of arbitration overcomes the possibility that collective bargaining will result in an agreed wage rate that is excessively high or low, for such agreement could be achieved only by coercion and coercion relies on the threat of conflict.

Arbitration is a less costly process of dispute resolution than conflict from the standpoint of the parties to the dispute. Conflict would be preferred to arbitration only by a party that would clearly be in the stronger position in the event of conflict. Collective bargaining does not work well when the parties are unevenly matched. The whole purpose of unions and the process of collective bargaining is to redress the imbalance of power that characterizes monopsony. But it is impossible to frame industrial relations legislation based on the principle of balanced strength in conflict that will ensure an appropriate balance of power in all cases. Replacement of conflict by arbitration immediately redresses the imbalance of bargaining strength in cases where that strength relies on ability to withstand conflict. The balance of power with arbitration depends on the respective abilities of the parties to persuade an arbitrator to decide in their favour. This in turn depends upon the criteria stipulated as guidelines for arbitrators. Proposed criteria are discussed in the next chapter. It is more feasible to frame legislation stipulating appropriate criteria for arbitration than it is to frame legislation governing the process of conflict that will ensure an appropriate balance of power between the parties.

Arbitration is clearly a more efficient process than conflict from the standpoint of third parties. A work stoppage causes costs and hardship for suppliers, customers, and complementary workers. I have discussed above the ways in which the process of strike and lock-out violates the public interest. Arbitration does not interrupt production and those costs are avoided. With appropriate criteria stipulated as guidelines for arbitrators, the outcome of arbitration can also be made to serve the public interest better than the diversity of outcomes that ensue from the process of conflict. Arbitration based on appropriate criteria would avoid both excessively high and excessively low wage rates. Such disparities are a major cause of inequity among workers and their removal would serve the objective of equity. Wage rates that are too high are a cause of unemployment and underemployment, which result in both inefficiency in the use of labour and inequity between those who receive high wages and those excluded from the occupations in question or charged unnecessarily high product prices. Arbitration that did not result in inefficiently high wage rates would overcome both the inefficiency and the inequity.

Arbitration is a quasi-judicial process. The model for the arbitration process is the law of contract and to some extent the law of tort. It is not difficult to conceive the resolution of a wage dispute in the employment contract as an extension of the process by which disputes arising from contracts are adjudicated in the courts. A contract is an agreement between two parties by which each accepts obligations to the other. The contract of employment is a contract. When dispute arises between the parties to a contract concerning the nature and extent of the obligations of one party to the other then, in the absence of agreed settlement, the aggrieved party may seek redress in the courts. The essence of the legal process is stipulation of the respective rights of parties in dispute about the meaning of a contract. The parties to a contract of employment may seek adjudication of its terms in the courts in the same way as the parties to any other contract. But the law of contract applies only to the explicit terms of a contract. The courts will not extend the terms of a contract beyond the obligations to which the parties have explicitly agreed. This is in accordance with the principle of freedom that no party should be bound by a contract to which it has not voluntarily agreed.

The basic problem with the indefinite period contract of employment is the impossibility of stating explicitly the wage rate that will be paid beyond some defined period. When the time comes to negotiate a wage rate for the next period, the parties are not already bound by explicit commitments that can be enforced by the courts, although they are effectively committed by the costs of mobility to a continuing contract between them. The dispute about the future wage rate does not concern enforcement of explicit promises already made and does not lie within the purview of the law of contract. It is for this reason that it becomes necessary to extend the law of contract by a quasi-judicial arbitration process that lies outside the courts proper. The courts are properly concerned only with integrity and only with the explicit terms of existing contracts. The arbitration process is concerned with efficiency and equity as well as integrity in extending the terms of existing contracts.

The law of tort is concerned with redressing the damages that one person may inflict on another outside the realm of any contract between them. The major concern of the public interest in collective bargaining is that both the process and the outcome may inflict harm on third parties principally by denying them free access to markets. The courts address issues of tort only when a plaintiff sues for redress. It is not feasible for all third parties adversely affected by contracts in the labour market to sue for damages, yet the public interest can be so significantly affected that it should not be ignored. The process of arbitration can be governed by criteria and guidelines that encompass consideration of the public interest as well as the interests of the principal parties. It is not necessary that third parties appear in the role of plaintiff. The principal parties are bound to be adversaries, for anything agreed between them is not subject to arbitration, so at least one of them will find it expedient to argue the public interest in the course of the proceedings. To the extent that the arbitrator is required to consider the public interest in adjudicating an issue, the arbitration process becomes an extension of the law of tort as well as of the law of contract.

Arbitration is already used in two situations to resolve disputes that arise from the collective bargaining process. The first occurs when the parties themselves agree to invoke arbitration to resolve their differences rather than face the costs of conflict. Provision for arbitration may be agreed before negotiations begin or it may be agreed only at the stage of dispute when conflict is imminent. In either case the parties themselves must agree on the procedure for selecting the arbitrator, the issues that he will be asked to arbitrate, and the criteria by which he will be asked to judge them.

Agreement to arbitration is not common in the private sector, even though it would avoid the costs of strike or lockout for both parties, because it is almost as difficult for the parties to agree about the arbitration procedure as it is for them to agree about the settlement. At the beginning of conflict the two parties may have quite different expectations about the outcome. If both anticipated the same outcome, they could agree without the need for conflict. The union will not agree to arbitration unless the criteria are such that the union expects an outcome from arbitration almost as favourable as it anticipates from conflict. The employer will not agree unless it expects an outcome almost as favourable to it. Each may be willing to accept less favourable terms from arbitration than it expects from conflict, because the avoided costs of conflict would be greater than the costs of arbitration, but their differences are still likely to preclude agreement about the arbitration procedure. The parties may agree to arbitration if the expected costs of conflict are high in relation to the difference between their offers. If both expect a long strike over a small dispute, any arbitrated settlement within the range bounded by their final offers would be better than conflict. But these are precisely the conditions under which an agreed settlement is likely without recourse to either conflict or arbitration.

Arbitration by agreement will arise in two situations, however. The first is when both parties' exaggerated expectations about the outcome of conflict are not only based on unrealistic beliefs concerning their coercive power but are also matched by conviction about the justice of their positions. Each will then expect to be as successful in persuading a neutral arbitrator as it would be in prevailing through conflict. They may then agree on a neutral form of arbitration. The second situation arises when one party clearly has the power to coerce the other. The weak party may then face the options of accepting an unfavourable settlement, suffering conflict that it will lose, or agreeing to arbitration on terms dictated by the strong party. The last may be the least unattractive option.

The possibility that one party may have the power to stipulate unfair conditions of arbitration could be overcome by statutory provision for the arbitration procedure. But if both parties must agree to arbitration, such a procedure would still be rarely used. The inefficiency and inequity of conflict arise both from the process and the outcome. Problems with the outcome could be overcome only if arbitration would achieve a different outcome. But one party would then prefer the outcome of conflict and refuse to agree to arbitration. Without agreement to invoke arbitration, the costs of the process of conflict would not be avoided.

Arbitration would become more common than conflict in the private sector only if a standard procedure and standard criteria were stipulated by statute and if either party could invoke arbitration without the agreement of the other. Currently both parties must agree to arbitration and arbitration is rare. If instead we required agreement to wage conflict rather than accept arbitration, conflict would be rare.

The second situation in which arbitration is used arises most commonly in the public sector when arbitration of a particular dispute is made mandatory by statute. This can be done either by designating in advance certain groups of workers who are denied the right to strike, or by emergency statute that terminates a strike or lock-out after it has begun, or prohibits it only when it is imminent, with provision in either case for compulsory arbitration.[3]

Thus our experience with arbitration is essentially of an *ad hoc* nature and a variety of provisions are used with respect to selection of arbitrators and the criteria by which they are asked to adjudicate. If we are to use arbitration instead of conflict throughout the labour market to resolve disputes arising from collective bargaining, then it will be necessary to establish a standard procedure for arbitration. One basic principle of the rule of law is that individuals should know the law, and the procedure and criteria used by the courts before they decide on actions that may become the subject of proceedings. In the negotiation phase of collective bargaining, arbitration rather than conflict would be the alternative to acceptance of the other party's offer. While it can never be known in advance precisely what decisions a court or arbitrator will make in a particular case, the more clearly the procedure is defined, the less the degree of uncertainty concerning the alternatives available to each party. The procedure must be stipulated by statute for one cannot rely on agreement between the parties about the criteria for arbitration. The parties may fail to agree or a strong party may impose its will on the other by coercion. If a standard form of arbitration is available to each party, neither can be coerced by the other. There is then no reason why the criteria of arbitration should not be modified at the request of the parties provided that they agree. Arbitration is intended to resolve disputes, not to override areas of voluntary agreement between the parties.

A further major reason for having a standard procedure for arbitration is that it would facilitate the accumulation of a body of case law. The courts are governed by both law and precedent. The availability of an extensive body of case law helps to ensure that comparable cases are judged comparably. This accords with the principles of equity. Knowledge of case law enables the parties to predict the decision of courts with greater certainty, which enhances the prospects of their reaching agreement. If the negotiating parties in collective bargaining could refer to a standard body of case law, they could predict the outcome of arbitration with greater certainty. The better that can be predicted, the greater is the prospect of their reaching agreement without recourse to arbitration.[4] Case law applies only to comparable situations and one cannot establish a meaningful body of case law if the criteria for arbitration differ from case to case.

The current procedures of our judicial system offer much valuable guidance to the framers of the legislation that would govern the quasi-judicial process of arbitration.[5] Arbitrators could be appointed by a process that parallels the appointment of judges. The parties in a legal case do not have the right to appoint their own judges, nor would disputing parties have the right to appoint their own arbitrators, though they would have comparable rights to object to a particular person for specified reasons. The rules governing evidence and argument may well have to be different in the less formal atmosphere of arbitration, but again the courts serve as the initial model. One important role of counsel in the judicial process is to encourage the disputing parties to agree so that a trial is unnecessary. A comparable role exists for mediation and conciliation in the collective bargaining process. Arbitration is a last resort. Agreement between the parties is always preferable if the agreement is genuinely voluntary. Provision for a standard form of arbitration itself protects the parties from coercion. Adjudication

is a costly process and the costs of our judicial system are
borne partly by taxpayers and partly by the parties in dispute.
Since one function of the arbitration process would be to protect the public interest, it is appropriate that part of the costs
be borne by taxpayers. It is, however, important that the parties to the dispute bear some of the costs in order to deter
the submission of trivial or frivolous disputes and to encourage settlement by agreement wherever possible.[6] One function
of the courts is to assign the burden of costs. A similar provision could exist in the arbitration process – the arbitrator
could assign the greater burden of costs to the party with the
more unreasonable case.

A considerable problem arises in determining the extent to
which arbitration should be binding. Clearly there is no point
in incurring the costs of the arbitration process if both parties
remain free to ignore the findings. But a process by which
either party could successfully seek arbitration, the effect of
which would be to impose on the other party a contract to
which it had never agreed, would violate the principle of freedom of contract. The solution to this problem lies in distinguishing the types of contracts discussed in previous chapters.

In the spot labour market contracts are of very short duration and there is no presumption that contracts will be renewed.
Such contracts cannot lead to arbitration. Defined period contracts have an explicit date of termination and the wage rate
and other conditions of employment are specified by agreement
when the contract is made. While the parties may negotiate a
subsequent period contract, if they fail to agree neither has
any obligation to the other when the period of the contract
expires. There is accordingly no issue to refer to arbitration.
Thus arbitration cannot be used to impose obligations on either
party against its will if the parties restrict themselves to spot
or defined period contracts. Arbitration arises only in the case
of the indefinite period contract.

The feature that distinguishes the indefinite period contract
from the defined period contract is the provision for liquidated damages in the event of withdrawal from the contract by
either party, with no explicit expiry date on the obligation to
pay such damages. If the employer is obliged to give notice of
termination, or compensation in lieu thereof, and that obligation does not automatically terminate at a defined expiry date,
then we have an indefinite period contract. If the employee is
required to give notice of termination, or participates in a pen-

sion plan without provision for full vesting of his rights on a defined expiry date, then the contract is for an indefinite term. The expectation of the parties to an indefinite term contract is that it will continue indefinitely. It is precisely the continuation of the obligations of one party to the other beyond the period for which remuneration is specified by agreement that gives rise to the issues that may lead to the need for arbitration. If a standard arbitration procedure is established in the labour market, the presumption would be that a contract is for an indefinite term unless the contract explicitly provides for the expiry of all obligations by either party to the other at the end of a defined period.

The basic form of the indefinite period contract leaves either party free to terminate it at will by honouring the specified obligations on termination. Remuneration must be specified at the outset but there may or may not be an agreed defined period for which the specified wage rate will apply. If there is no such defined period, the wage rate may be renegotiated at any time and either party should be able to seek arbitration in the event of failure to agree. The arbitrator's ruling would then specify the period for which his judgment would remain valid and the issue could not be resubmitted for arbitration during that period. If the initial wage rate is agreed for a defined period, the issue could not be taken to arbitration until the expiry of that period. Thus all such contracts would have a defined period during which the current wage rate would remain valid after the first arbitration if not before. If either party is unwilling to accept continuation of the contract at the arbitrated wage rate, that party is free to terminate it by observing the procedure for termination and paying any liquidated damages. Thus arbitration could not impose continuing binding obligations on either party against its will. This is in accordance with the principle of freedom that no party can be bound by a contract to which it has not agreed. Arbitration would thus overcome the basic ambiguity of the indefinite period contract. When liquidated damages are payable by a party who withdraws from a contract, but there is failure to agree on its continuing terms, it is not clear which party has withdrawn. The arbitrator would specify the continuing terms and the party that refuses to accept them would then be the one terminating the contract and liable for the specified damages.

An arbitrator's judgment may be binding on the parties and give rise to continuing binding obligations, without violating the principles of freedom, if the parties agree in advance to accept binding arbitration. Some contracts do not permit the employer to terminate employment at will. He may be required to show cause for dismissing an employee or be liable for damages for wrongful dismissal. Various degrees of job security may be provided for in the employment contract, the extreme case being those that provide tenure for life or until retirement. The employer may be required to show cause in a prescribed way before he can terminate such a contract. Job security is valuable to the employee but restricts the employer's freedom of action. When the parties agree to encompass job security in a contract it will typically be in exchange for a lower wage rate. By accepting a lower wage rate than would be available in some other employment not providing job security, the employee essentially purchases job insurance from the employer. The paradox then arises that the employee has purchased long-term security of employment at a future wage rate yet to be specified. The promise of job security is implicitly a promise of continued employment at a "fair" wage rate. There would clearly be a breach of integrity if an employer enticed an employee to accept a lower wage rate in exchange for job security and subsequently insisted that the real wage rate in question be permitted to fall unreasonably with inflation. The purpose of arbitration is to specify a "fair" wage rate when the parties cannot reach agreement. Commitment by an employer to job security at a fair wage is then implicitly commitment to job security at an arbitrated wage. Arbitration may then be binding for the only "freedom" that is violated is freedom to perpetrate a breach of integrity.

Thus the extent to which arbitration is binding on the employer will depend on the form of the contract. Arbitration does not arise with spot or defined period contracts. In the case of the indefinite period contract, arbitration specifies the wage rate for the ensuing period. If the contract permits the employer to withdraw at will, he is not bound by a wage rate he does not agree to pay. If the contract denies him freedom to withdraw, then the arbitrated wage rate binds him to the extent that he has voluntarily committed himself to an obligation of continuing employment. Arbitration is not binding on the employee in the sense that he can be required to continue in employment, for the worker is always free to resign, though perhaps at the expense of suffering the costs of liquidated damages. The employee is, however, denied freedom to renegotiate the wage rate during the period specified for the arbitrated wage. Parties who voluntarily enter contracts implicitly agree subsequently to be bound by the judgment of courts according to the law of contract. When a standard procedure for arbitration is established, they similarly implicitly agree to be bound by the judgment of arbitrators concerning the future revision of the wage rate in the light of changing circumstances.

Thus it is possible to establish a standard arbitration procedure that preserves individual freedom, the right to enter or refrain from entering contracts, the right to bargain and to bargain collectively, the right to make any contract that is mutually agreed and to have it enforced, while relieving the parties from the costs of conflict and coercion by the threat of conflict, and the society as a whole from the inefficiencies and inequities of a collective bargaining system based on trial by conflict.

The public sector suffers from the same deficiencies of the collective bargaining process as the private sector but often in a more extreme form. Arbitration can work as well in one sector as in the other. The extreme cost of conflict in the public sector has on many occasions persuaded our society to use arbitration, though often on an *ad hoc* and emergency basis. No *ad hoc* measures would be needed with a standard arbitration system and the same procedures could apply to both sectors. There is no reason why the public and private sectors should be treated differently for the public interest in efficiency, equity, and integrity applies to both.[7] If appropriate criteria for arbitration are established, there should be no need for recourse to regulation of wages by controls or guidelines either of a permanent form or as temporary emergency expedients. Only in such extreme circumstances as wartime might exceptional measures become necessary.

While not denying legitimate scope for the use of spot or defined period contracts, we must conclude that the indefinite period contract based on collective bargaining, with recourse to arbitration when the stage of dispute is reached, best satisfies the principles and criteria. It remains only to recommend the sequence by which such a system might be established.

CHAPTER EIGHT

Conclusions and Recommendations

The basic recommendations to which this study leads should be clear from the analysis contained in previous chapters. There is no reason to interfere in any way with the operation of the labour market in spot or defined period contracts. When the parties to a contract agree to limit the period of their relationship, and the terms of the contract are clearly specified in advance, no issues affecting the public interest arise and normal market forces operate effectively. The law of contract suffices to enforce contracts voluntarily made.

The bulk of the labour market, however, relies on the indefinite period contract and does so for good reason. The high costs of search, training, and mobility make it appropriate that employers and employees should be committed to each other by a continuing relationship. Such ongoing contracts do not imply indenture nor necessarily tenure, and provision exists for either party to terminate the relationship in a prescribed way with costs of termination that effectively constitute liquidated damages. An efficient degree of mobility of labour requires that different contracts of employment provide for different levels of commitment by the parties to each other.

All indefinite period contracts suffer from one major problem, however, and it is the root cause of the problems addressed in this study. It is impossible to foresee changing economic circumstances far into the future and it is accordingly impossible to prescribe at the outset of an indefinite period contract the wage rates and other conditions of employment that will prevail throughout its life. The fundamental paradox is inevitable that both parties have some commitment to continuation of a contract of employment, with no clear agreement of the continuing terms of the contract to which they are committed. There must be some procedure by which the wage rate can be revised from time to time.

In the absence of any other procedure, the employer states the wage rate at which he is willing to continue employment. Such power provides scope for the exploitation of a captive labour force and an alternative system has evolved in which workers organize into unions and bargain collectively with their employers. Collective bargaining may result in a negotiated settlement to which both parties voluntarily agree. But in the absence of agreement the dispute is resolved by conflict. The procedure of conflict by strike and lock-out is an inefficient and inequitable process. There is no reason to believe that it always results in a satisfactory outcome, and the anticipation of an unsatisfactory outcome makes possible the achievement of unsatisfactory "agreed" settlements by coercion.

The resolution of disputes arising from the collective bargaining process is the basic problem and the recommendation is that such disputes be resolved by arbitration rather than by the conflict of strike or lock-out. Arbitration would be used only when the normal process of collective bargaining fails to result in agreement. It would not replace freedom of contract in the labour market and would not be a system of wage control. It would only replace resolution by conflict when the market and collective bargaining fail. In order to implement this recommendation while making minimum necessary changes to a society based on individual freedom and freedom of contract, the following specific recommendations are made.

RECOMMENDATIONS

1 *Establishment of an Arbitration Service.* The first recommendation is that there be provision by statute for the establishment of an arbitration service to resolve disputes arising from collective bargaining about the continuing terms of indefinite period contracts in both the public and private sectors.[1]

Arbitration is a quasi-judicial process. Our system of courts is a public service provided and operated by government. A system of arbitration tribunals should be similarly structured as a public service established by government with arbitrators appointed by government. The judicial system should serve as the model for the arbitration system, though there are important differences and it is not necessary that arbitrators be lawyers by training and background. The criteria for dispute resolution are not the same as those of the law of contract and tort. The relevant skills needed by arbitrators could be acquired by specialists in industrial relations and economics as well as by specialists in law. Whatever his background, an arbitrator would need to acquire an understanding of the relevant parts of other disciplines. Arbitration is not a trial, and the rules of procedure in arbitration cases may well differ from those used in the courts proper. We now have enough experience of arbitration to guide us in establishing such an arbitration service by statute with prescribed criteria and rules of procedure.[2] Such a statute could, of course, be amended from time to time in the light of experience.

The responsibility of arbitrators is great and implementation of the proposed criteria will be difficult. The principle of efficiency requires that arbitrators assess the extent of the shortage or surplus of labour of particular types and such information is not readily available. The extent to which unemployment and underemployment exist among workers with particular skills in a particular location, and the effect that a change in the wage rate would have are difficult matters to measure and interpret statistically. Such issues are controversial even among specialists in the study of labour markets. The parties, of course, have an interest in presenting the arbitrator with relevant evidence and argument, but small businesses and weak unions are unlikely to be able to do so thoroughly. In all cases the parties have the incentive to select evidence most favourable to themselves and to place upon such evidence biased interpretation. Thus the arbitrator will be confronted by the parties with incomplete and conflicting evidence and argument, some valid, some false, and some exaggerated. Assessing such evidence to distil from it the basis of a sound judgment will often be very difficult. Arbitrators will need help from competent, independent experts and it is therefore proposed that the arbitration service include a central research staff.

The research staff, including specialists in statistics, economics, econometrics, industrial relations, and law, would fulfil a number of important functions. It would maintain a complete, up-to-date reference library of the relevant available data on current wage rates, unemployment and related labour market conditions, and the case law of previous judgments. When a case is presented for arbitration, the submissions of the two parties would go first to the research staff for assessment. The arbitrator would then be confronted with three documents, the submissions of the two parties and the brief from the research staff commenting on the validity of the submissions and adding other relevant information. The brief by the research staff should be provided to the parties before the hearing. If the need for further evidence should arise during the hearing, the arbitrator would be able to refer back to the research staff for additional information.

The extent to which the research staff could influence the outcome of arbitration is clearly a delicate issue. Some may fear that the staff could become a bureaucracy practising disguised wage control by recommending a decision in each case that the arbitrator would simply ratify. Similar fears exist throughout our legal system, though they are typically either without foundation or exaggerated. The lay Justice of the Peace relies on the Clerk of the Court for advice on matters of law, but remains responsible for rendering his own independent judgment. Expert witnesses are commonly used in trials, but the influence of their opinions on the outcome is at the discretion of the judge and jury. Arbitrators would similarly be responsible for deciding the weight that they should place on the evidence presented by the research staff. That evidence would be subject to counter argument by the parties during the hearing. The system is designed to contain the safeguards of checks and balances. The research staff provide the arbitrator with relevant information. The arbitrator decides the extent to which he should attach weight to the arguments of the two parties and the information provided by the research staff. The arbitrator's judgment becomes part of the case law, and the precedents of previous arbitrators' judgments are a crucial part of the information assembled by the research staff. The emerging body of case law is monitored by government and any trends deemed contrary to the public interest can be changed by statutory amendment to the stated criteria.

No system that relies on human judgment is ever perfect. There can be no guarantee that the outcome of every case is precisely right, for there is no single precisely right answer to each issue nor would there be any way to determine the right answer if there were one. If we knew the right answer, to which an arbitrator's judgment could be compared, there would be no need for the arbitrator. But the proposed system does provide a method to determine wage rates in a consistent, balanced, and fair way that would be a vast improvement on the outcome of separate conflict in each case, which is the process that currently determines the structure of wage rates.

2 *Statutory Criteria for Arbitration.* The second recommendation is that the criteria for arbitration be stated in the statute that establishes the arbitration service.

The fundamental principles of the rule of law require that all persons be bound by the same rules and that all know what those rules are. If arbitration is to be governed by the principles of justice, it is important that the criteria for arbitration be the same in different cases. Statute law evolved to replace the arbitrary opinions of judges concerning the nature of justice. In the past, voluntary arbitration has been based on different criteria in different cases, the criteria in each case being agreed by the parties or left for the individual arbitrator to decide. Only if the criteria for wage settlements are stated by statute can we avoid the uncertainty and diversity that result when individual arbitrators are left to exercise their own opinions. Arbitration must involve judgment concerning the circumstances of the particular case, but arbitration need not be, and should not be, totally arbitrary. The right to arbitration implies the right to arbitration according to standard known criteria.[3]

The purpose of an arbitration service is to serve the public interest in having both efficient wage rates and an equitable distribution of income. The criteria of what constitutes the public interest is a matter of social choice and the making of social choice is the function of government. This study has argued that the emphasis should be placed on the role of the wage rate as the price charged the employer for the use of labour rather than on its role as the income of the worker. The criterion of efficiency should take precedence over the criterion of equity in wage arbitration. That precedence will be observed only if it is clearly required by statute. It is the function of the tax and transfer system to redress any inequity in the distribution of income that results from efficient wages. Income redistribution is the direct responsibility of government, not arbitrators.

The following are the recommended criteria, in order of importance.

i) *Integrity.* The fundamental principle of freedom of contract requires that any commitment into which a party enters voluntarily should be honoured and that no party should be bound by a commitment to which he has not voluntarily agreed. Thus arbitration cannot be used to extend or modify the terms of spot or defined period contracts that the parties intended to expire on a defined date. But commitment to an indefinite period contract, and all commitments for job security and provision for liquidated damages in the event of default that such a contract may contain, are voluntary commitments to the continuation of employment at a fair wage rate and integrity requires that they be honoured and enforced.

ii) *Efficiency.* While it must not be used to condone a breach of integrity, the most important criterion in arbitrating wage rates is the achievement of efficiency in the use of our labour resources. This requires that the wage rate be viewed principally as the price society charges the employer for the use of a unit of labour. Each unit of labour should be priced at a wage rate that properly reflects its alternative value to society.[4] Scarcity of particular skills justifies a high price to encourage economy in the use of those skills. High cost of acquiring human capital through investment in education and training justifies a correspondingly high wage rate both to encourage economy in the use of expensive human capital and to encourage investment in its acquisition.

The composition of the labour force is never in long-run equilibrium. If it were, the wage rates indicated by the current relative scarcity of different skills would also reflect the relative costs of their acquisition. When the demand for particular skills grows, there will be a short-run shortage of such skills. The wage rate indicated by the immediate scarcity will be higher than that indicated by the cost of investment in such skills. The arbitrated wage rates should be between these levels, not for reasons of compromise but for reasons of efficiency. A wage rate above the long-run equilibrium level is needed to encourage increased investment in the relevant human capital, but a wage rate that fully reflects the immediate scarcity may encourage excessive training in such skills leading to a surplus of such labour in future. The objective of the arbitrator should be to set a wage rate that will lead to the smooth and orderly adjustment of the number of workers possessing such skills, but not to instability in either the numbers of new recruits undertaking the relevant training or in the relevant wage rate in future years. When the demand for a particular skill declines, the immediate surplus of such workers will indicate a wage rate below the level needed to maintain a flow of new workers into the occupation. Again the arbitrated wage rate must be between those levels and be such as to lead to a smooth and orderly decline in the numbers undertaking the relevant training without giving rise to future instability.

The need to encourage full and efficient use of the existing stock of workers with a particular skill, without encouraging undue expansion or decline in the rate of new investment in the relevant human capital, may call for temporarily high or low wage rates. When the wage rates indicated by short-run and long-run considerations diverge greatly, the arbitrated wage rate should be set for a short period of perhaps one year to permit readjustment in the near future. When the two indicated wage rates are very close, indicating that the particular submarket is close to long-run equilibrium, the arbitrated wage rate may be set for a longer period of perhaps three years, with possible provision for automatic adjustment in the second and third years to reflect inflation.

Just as scarcity of particular skills and high costs of training indicate that efficient wage rates should be high, so does a surplus of labour and low cost of investment in human capital indicate that the efficient wage rate should be low.[5] A surplus of labour of a particular type, which manifests itself as a high rate of unemployment among such workers, is clear evidence to the arbitrator that the current real wage rate is too high and should be permitted to fall to encourage the employment of labour whose alternative value to society is very low. Only in this way could we achieve full utilization of the labour force and give those currently unemployed access to an expanded labour market.

Efficiency requires an optimum degree of mobility among occupations. The setting of wage rates by arbitration that are designed to result in neither surplus nor shortage of workers with the relevant skills will enhance the prospect that individual workers could find alternative employment and employers could find alternative workers. The actual extent of mobility will be constrained by the costs thereof. An inefficiently high degree of mobility will be achieved if the wage rates differ widely in two occupations between which workers can move freely or employers practise substitution. Thus it is important for reasons of efficiency that arbitrators pay due attention to prevailing wage rates in comparable occupations.

iii) *Equity*. While the arbitrator is principally concerned with efficiency, and equity in the distribution of income is the proper concern of the tax and transfer payment system, the arbitrator must be concerned with equity in the relative wage rates of different occupations. Income redistribution may reduce the magnitude of the differences between different wage rates, but it will not reverse the relative incomes of different workers. The arbitrator must be guided by prevailing wage rates in other occupations to ensure that his judgment does not violate the principles of either horizontal or vertical equity. Horizontal equity requires that workers in comparable occupations be remunerated with comparable wage rates. Vertical equity requires that workers whose jobs involve high levels of skill, responsibility, danger, or unpleasantness receive higher wage rates than those whose jobs do not. The arbitrator should be guided by the evidence of other prevailing wage rates in setting a wage that will leave the occupation in question in a proper relationship to other occupations.

The arbitrator must also be guided by considerations of equity between workers in the occupation in question and the public at large. A high rate of unemployment may be compatible with a wage rate in the occupation in question that is either inequitably low or inequitably high. When the only alternative to previous acceptance of an inequitably low wage rate was unemployment, workers may have been coerced into accepting a wage rate that is inequitably low by comparison with the wage rates prevailing in other occupations. At the same time the wage rate in question is inequitably high by comparison with the plight of the comparably qualified unemployed. The worker cannot be worse off than the unemployed for he always has the option of leaving his current employment and becoming unemployed instead, while the person currently unemployed does not have the choice. The arbitrator may thus be confronted with the dilemma that wage rates that are too high in other occupations are causing a high level of unemployment, which in turn has led to a wage rate in the occupation in question that is inequitably low. We do not live in a perfect world. The power of the arbitrator is limited to setting the wage rate in the occupation currently before him. Since he cannot redress inequities elsewhere, he cannot possibly achieve total equity between the workers before him and all other members of society, when the others are not equitably related to each other. The most that the arbitrator can do when confronted with such conflicting evidence is to render a reasonable second-best judgment.

As the arbitration system becomes established, and results through a series of cases in the redressing of any major cases of inequity in the labour market and the wider society, the problem of conflicting evidence should lessen.

iv) *Precedent*. The arbitrator should be guided, but not bound, by the precedents of previously arbitrated cases. The importance of the observance of precedent is that it permits the accumulation of a body of case law. If justice is to dispensed by the arbitration service, it is vital that it be dispensed consistently.[6] The criteria of arbitration should be established by statute and the arbitration service should be responsible to the elected government. While the service should enjoy a degree of independence comparable with that of the judiciary, government is the ultimate arbiter of the public interest. Government would not interfere in the arbitration of particular cases. Any such intervention would destroy the credibility of the process, particularly when it is used for arbitration in the public sector. But when clear practices emerge in the case law from the interpretations that arbitrators place upon the statutory criteria, government must either take responsibility for those practices or override them by amendment to the statute. The process by which legislation can override case law, while there is no scope for political interference in particular cases, requires that a clear body of case law should emerge and that can happen only by the observance of precedent.

A consistent body of case law is vital to the important function of the arbitration process in cases that do not reach the stage of arbitration. Once the system is established, arbitration will be the alternative to agreement. With a clear body of case law the parties can predict the outcome of arbitration. It will not then be possible to secure agreement of both parties to a contract that differs significantly from what would result from arbitration. Settlements reached by agreement will then accord with the same criteria as those that govern the arbitration process. The vast majority of disputes in matters of law do not reach the courts precisely because the parties can predict the decision of the court and abide by it without need for a trial. We can similarly expect that as the body of case law under the arbitration process accumulates, the vast majority of disputes will be resolved by agreement without the need for arbitration.[7]

Although the accumulation of case law is an important function of the arbitration process, and it requires the observance of precedent, precedents should not be strictly binding on the arbitrator. In an imperfect world arbitrators must make second-best judgments. This will be particularly true of the first judgments under the new process. With the passage of time the grossest inefficiencies and inequities in the structure of wage rates that give rise to the need for second-best judgment will be ameliorated. Such second-best judgments should not become binding precedents after they have ceased to be either necessary or appropriate.

3 *The Right of Workers to Organize.* The third recommendation is that any group of workers currently employed under an indefinite period contract have the right to form a union.

This recommendation requires no change in current policy. Different groups or workers form associations of various kinds for the purpose of negotiating wage rates and conditions of employment. Provision is already made for the procedure by which any group may form a trade union. There is no reason why the current variety of forms of association should not continue to exist. Any form of organization that the members consider satisfactory gives rise to no problems provided that the option of forming a trade union in the strict sense is available and the power of a trade union is such as to afford reasonable assurance of a reasonable outcome.

Workers have the right to negotiate their conditions of employment, to bargain, and to bargain collectively. But the power to bargain effectively requires the power to force an employer to agree to a reasonable contract. The current right to strike is of little value to a group of workers who would be in a very weak position in the event of conflict with their employer. There is little point in forming a union if the union would have no effective power. The right to organize and bargain collectively is meaningful only when there is a last resort procedure that affords assurance of a reasonable outcome for both the weak and the strong. The current right to organize will become meaningful in that sense when a union has the right to invoke arbitration. The existence of that option will enhance the prospects for other forms of organizations to achieve acceptable wage rates and conditions of employment.

Provision for arbitration may well result in the formation of more unions, particularly in occupations where unions do not currently exist because they would be too weak to be effective. An increase in unionization would not in itself be a problem, but it may be feared that contraction of the nonunionized labour market would reduce the size of the observable market sector that often serves to guide arbitrators about market trends. The availability of arbitration may thus reduce the availability of relevant evidence to guide arbitrators. That fear may well prove unfounded, however. Unions would be formed only when it is anticipated that arbitration would achieve a higher wage rate. If arbitrators set appropriate wage rates, it follows that the wage rates before unionization were too low and would have provided poor guidance for arbitrators about what comparable wage rates should be. Proper guidance could only come from nonunionized submarkets in which the prevailing wage is approximately what it would be if arbitrated. These are precisely the cases in which there would be no incentive to form unions and the ones that may be expected to remain nonunionized. The ready availability of the process of unionization and arbitration should serve to persuade employers to pay wage rates comparable to arbitrated rates without the need for unionization. Once appropriate wage rates become inevitable there is incentive to agree to them without need for the process of bargaining and arbitration. Thus the extent to which the availability of arbitration would in fact lead to a significant increase in unionization is questionable. But we could expect that the remaining nonunionized sector would become a much better source of guidance for arbitrators. In effect the arbitrators would be guided by market expectations of what arbitrators would decide. When each sector observes and emulates the other, the extent of inequitable disparities in wage rates between the unionized and nonunionized sectors should be reduced.

4 *The Right to Arbitration.* The fourth recommendation is that when a group of workers have formed a trade union in the specified sense, either the union or the employer have the right to call for arbitration if negotiation fails to result in agreement.[8]

The current procedures for negotiation with provision for

mediation or conciliation may continue with little if any change. If agreement is not achieved, the final stage of the current process is the right to strike or lock-out. This recommendation provides instead for the right to arbitration. In the case of workers whose current conditions of employment are not specified in a contract, the process of negotiation may begin at any time. After a defined period for negotiation and conciliation there should be the right to arbitration if agreement has not been reached. When the current conditions are stated in a contract, the right to arbitration should exist only on the expiry of that contract. In either event the arbitrator should decide the wage rate and other conditions of employment and the period for which his judgment will remain valid. The right to subsequent arbitration should arise only on the expiry of that period. It is recommended that the period for an arbitrated settlement be not less than one year nor more than three years. If the parties agree at the outset of the arbitration process on the period for which an arbitrated settlement is sought, then the arbitrator should respect that agreement. If there is no agreement, the period should be at the arbitrator's discretion.

Throughout this discussion of the labour market, I have focused on the wage rate as the critical contentious issue. It is not, however, the only matter decided by collective bargaining and would not be the only issue subject to arbitration. Such items as hours of work, overtime rates, paid vacations, paid sick leave, insurance, and pension plans are other dimensions of remuneration. Issues concerning working conditions, health, and safety are also negotiated where they are not prescribed by statute. The very nature of the employment contract may be changed by negotiation if there is dispute about job security or other dimensions of the liquidated damages that characterize the indefinite period contract. The extent to which such issues may be subject to arbitration is governed by the recommended criteria.

Benefits that are in the nature of remuneration present little problem. Longer paid vacations and greater employer contributions to pension plans, for example, clearly raise the cost of labour to the employer. Both parties recognize that there is a trade-off between such items of remuneration and the wage rate. If the arbitrator is asked to adjudicate disputed items, there is no reason why he should not do so. His principle concern is to establish an appropriate figure for the total cost of employing the type of labour in question. Disputes about the composition of that total can be arbitrated in the light of the desires and arguments presented by the parties and by reference to prevailing standards in comparable occupations. If the arbitrator's judgment is such that both parties would have preferred a different composition, they are free to change it by agreement. Arbitration is not wage control. Whatever an arbitrator decides in resolving a dispute can subsequently be changed by agreement between the parties. The arbitrated settlement is intended only to state the respective rights of the two parties that would prevail in the absence of agreement between them to the contrary.

Disputes concerning the nature of the employment contract itself could present problems, however, for they could involve violation of the principle of integrity. A union may seek greater job security for its members through the collective bargaining process. It may, for example, ask for guarantees against layoffs, longer periods of notice of termination of employment, or higher severance settlements. If an arbitrator granted such requests, however, the employer would become bound by contractual obligations to which he had never agreed. The principle of integrity requires that arbitration cannot be binding on either party because either should be free to terminate employment in a way to which it had agreed and on the payment of liquidated damages to which it had agreed. The principle of integrity should severely limit the extent to which arbitration can bind either party to a contract with conditions of termination to which that party has never agreed. This is important not only because of the inherent justice of the principle of integrity, but because it is vital to the efficiency of the labour market. If unemployment is to be reduced, new jobs must be created. New jobs arise either in expanding firms or in new firms. Expansion and new ventures are often risky and entrepreneurs are willing to undertake them only when the maximum extent of their losses is predictable. Some new ventures fail and close. If an employer were forced by arbitration to offer a greater degree of job security, or greater compensation for termination of employment, maximum losses would increase. Entrepreneurs will be more reluctant to undertake risky new ventures once the precedent and fear are created than a venture may be made more costly to terminate than was expected when it was begun. If we are not to discourage the creation of new jobs, it is vital that the principle of integrity be strictly observed.

This does not, of course, mean that provisions for job security can never be changed once the arbitration service is established. The discussion of liquidated damages in chapter 3 concluded that greater job security, or higher liquidated damages payable by the employer on dismissal, will be accompanied by a lower wage rate. Once the arbitrator has established the appropriate wage rate in the light of the current provisions for liquidated damages, there is no reason why the parties should not negotiate and agree to greater damages, or greater job security, in exchange for an appropriate reduction in the wage rate. The wage reduction necessary to persuade the employer to agree would, of course, have to be greater in a new and risky venture than it would be in a well-established firm with an apparently secure future. The agreed liquidated damages would be the relevant frame of reference at the next arbitration.

5 *Withdrawal of the Right to Strike and Lock-out.* The fifth recommendation is that the right of a union to strike and the right of an employer to lock-out be withdrawn when the right to arbitration becomes effective. Consideration should be given to an initial three year moratorium on the right to strike and lock-out, with provision for review of the arbitration process during the third year. If the process is working satisfactorily, the right to strike and lock-out should then be abolished.

Arbitration is intended to be an alternative to conflict by strike and lock-out. Clearly if either party is to enjoy the right to arbitration, the other cannot retain the right to wage conflict. Denial of the right to strike does not commit the worker to continued service against his will. Any worker remains free to terminate his employment under the conditions prescribed in his contract of employment. Denial of the right to lock-out does not deny the employer the right to terminate employment. The employer retains the right to dismiss workers or to lay-off workers by the procedures specified in the contract. Strikes and lock-outs differ from resignations and dismissals in that the former are temporary suspensions of the employment relationship designed to impose pressure on the other party to yield in the process of negotiation. The right to wage conflict by such means is incompatible with arbitration.

6 *Review of Income Redistribution Policies.* The sixth recommendation is that there be a comprehensive review of current

income redistribution policies with a view both to simplifying current practice and to making such changes as may be appropriate for a system of arbitrated wage disputes.

We currently use wage rates in an effort to satisfy two incompatible purposes, and succeed in neither. On the one hand, the wage rate is the price charged the employer for the use of labour services. The purpose of that price is to ration a scarce valuable resource. On the other hand, the wage rate is the income of the worker. The objective then is to achieve an equitable distribution of income. The criterion of efficiency requires that wage rates be used principally for the former purpose and the second recommendation proposed this criterion for the arbitration service. Adoption of this criterion will inevitably mean that the wage rate of highly productive workers with skills in scarce supply will be very much higher than the wage rate of workers with skills in abundant supply. While the criterion of equity in arbitration should mean that no worker is paid more than another who deserves more, the magnitudes of the differences among wage rates may well be greater than our sense of equity in the distribution of income would find acceptable. In particular the efficient wage rate of unskilled and inexperienced workers will be very low if it is to reflect the abundant supply of such workers and achieve employment for those whose potential labour services are currently wasted in unemployment.

There will accordingly be need for a tax and transfer system designed to transfer income from high wage earners to low wage earners. Income supplements will be needed for low wage earners which may be accomplished best by a negative income tax. A system that achieves full employment with income supplements for low wage earners will be both more efficient and more equitable than a system that achieves adequate wages for some, subsidized wages for some, and unemployment insurance or welfare relief for the significant number consigned to idleness.

The ability of society to alleviate poverty by income redistribution depends on the total income generated by the society. The recommendations have been designed to generate income efficiently. The achievement of full and efficient utilization of our labour resources will clearly enhance our ability to mitigate poverty. But the use of efficient wage rates will not itself achieve equity in the distribution of income. It is accordingly recommended that the host of current income redistribution policies be reviewed and consolidated into a single system designed to achieve equity in the distribution of income by tax and transfer policy when relative wage rates are used to achieve efficiency.

7 *Abolition of the Minimum Wage.* The seventh recommendation is that the minimum wage law be repealed. This recommendation should be implemented following the review of the arbitration process in the third year that was proposed in the fifth recommendation.

The current minimum wage law does not guarantee a minimum wage, it only prohibits employment at less than the minimum wage. It is intended both to limit the exercise of monopsony power and to establish a lower limit for the income of any employed person. The former objective will be achieved by arbitration and the latter by income redistribution. Most workers currently protected by the minimum wage are not unionized, for there is little point in forming a union that would not have the means to confront a powerful employer successfully. The right to arbitration makes strike funds unnecessary. The threat of unionization and possible strike is not currently credible for low wage workers, but the threat of unionization to invoke arbitration will be credible. If the implicit threat is credible, it will not be necessary for all such workers to form unions.

A minimum wage would be incompatible with the responsibility of arbitrators to set efficient wages. Equity will be better achieved by a minimum income that protects all members of the labour force. It would be more comprehensive and less discriminatory than a minimum wage that protects only those fortunate enough to find employment, while denying others the right to sell their labour for wages some employer is willing to pay. It is recommended that the minimum wage be abolished after three years rather than immediately to ensure that the system of arbitration and particularly the system of income redistribution that replace it are well established.

CONCLUSIONS

If the above recommendations are adopted, the arbitration service and a comprehensive tax and transfer system will be in full operation by the end of the three year transition phase. It should then be possible to make the system permanent and strikes and lock-outs will become matters of only historical interest.

The proposed system offers the prospect of full and efficient utilization of our labour resources, uninterrupted production, and equity in the distribution of income. Excessive power in the labour market will be curtailed. Workers who would be in a weak position to wage conflict with their employers will be able to organize and seek arbitration on the same terms as other workers. The availability of arbitration will make it impossible for strong employers to exploit workers by coercing them into accepting wage rates that are unreasonably low. At the same time employers who depend on workers organized into strong unions will be freed from the strike threat. It will no longer be possible for a powerful union to hold the employer and the public to ransom in order to achieve a wage rate that is inefficiently and inequitably high. Workers in the public and private sectors will be protected by the same availability of arbitration based on the same criteria. While the arbitration service will enjoy freedom from political interference comparable with that enjoyed by the judiciary, government will be responsible for the statutory criteria governing the arbitration process and for the tax and transfer system that couples equity in the distribution of income with wage rates that price the use of labour services at levels that reflect the relative scarcity of workers with different skills and the alternative value of their services to society. All potential workers and customers will have access to markets, freedom to arrange their affairs through voluntary contracts, and to play a full role in the economic society. The greater efficiency in the use of our labour resources will generate the additional income that will make possible the income redistribution system that will alleviate poverty equitably across the society. The principles of freedom and voluntary contract will be retained and become available to all. There will be no need for periodic recourse to crude emergency measures of mandatory wage controls.

The proposed system promises much. It does not, of course, solve all our economic and social problems, nor will it be free from continuous controversy concerning the details of its control and operations. Such controversy will be focused in the political arena where it belongs. The system is not a blueprint for utopia, but it does offer very significant advantages over our current system and achieves them by a minimum necessary step in the evolution of our economic system.

All that adoption of these proposals requires is the wit to recognize facts and the will to act. Perfectly competitive markets are ideal but rare. In the modern world firms are large and the public sector is large, labour is specialized and mobility is costly. The only viable options are unfettered monopsony power, which is grossly inequitable; collective bargaining with dispute resolution by conflict, which is both inefficient and inequitable; government regulation, which is inflexible, inefficient, and violates our principles of personal freedom; or arbitration. We have known for centuries that a judicial system based on the rule of law is superior to private feud based on trial by combat. It is now time to recognize that a quasi-judicial process of arbitration is similarly superior to dispute resolution by conflict when the conditions necessary for the efficient operation of competitive free market forces are neither present nor possible.

Notes

1 Riddell, *Canadian Labour Relations*, 65.
2 Ibid., 5.
3 Freeman and Medoff, *What Do Unions Do?*, chapter 15.
4 The extent to which unions achieve higher wages is discussed in chapter 4.
5 Riddell, *Canadian Labour Relations*, 13.
6 Kumar, "Union Growth in Canada," 105.
7 Ibid., 104–5.
8 Riddell, *Canadian Labour Relations*, 12–13.
9 Krahn and Lowe, "Public Attitudes Towards Unions."
10 Riddell, *Canadian Labour Relations*, 13.
11 Kumar, "Union Growth in Canada", 105.
12 Riddell, *Canadian Labour Relations*, 12.
13 Ibid., 13.
14 The following examples illustrate the consensus in the literature about the adverse effects of unions:
"their activities necessarily reduce the productivity of labor all around and therefore also the general level of real wages; because, if union action succeeds in reducing the number of workers in the highly-paid jobs and in increasing the number of those who have to stay in the less remunerative ones, the result may be that the overall average will be lower. It is, in fact, more than likely that, in countries where unions are very strong, the general level of real wages is lower than it would otherwise be. This is certainly true ... where union policy is strengthened by the general use of restrictive practices of a 'make-work' character" (Hayek, *Tiger by the Tail*, 72).

"If the union is viewed solely in terms of its effect on the economy, it must in my opinion be considered an obstacle to the optimum performance of our economic system. It alters the wage structure in a way that impedes the growth of employment in sectors of the economy where productivity and income are naturally high and that leaves too much labour in low-income sectors of the economy like southern agriculture and the least skilled service trades. It benefits most those workers who would in any case be relatively well off, and while some of this gain may be at the expense of the owners of capital, most of it must be at the expense of consumers and the lower-paid workers" (Rees, *Economics of Trade Unions*, 186).

"On the one side, many economists view unions largely as monopolies in the labor market whose primary economic impact is to raise members' wages at the expense of unorganized labor and of the efficient functioning of the economy. These analysts stress the adverse effects of union work rules on productivity, the loss of employment in the organized sector due to union wage effects, and the consequent crowding of the nonunion sector with displaced workers ... Because monopolistic wage increases are socially harmful – in that they can be expected to induce both inefficiency and inequality – most economic studies, implicitly or explicitly, have judged unions as being a negative force in society ... As monopoly institutions, unions reduce society's output in three ways. First, union-won wage increases cause a misallocation of resources by inducing organized firms to hire fewer workers, to use more capital per worker, and to hire workers of higher quality then is socially optimal. Second, strikes called to force management to accept union demands reduce gross national product. Third, union contract provisions – such as limits on the loads that can be handled by workers, restrictions on tasks performed, and featherbedding – lower the productivity of labor and capital" (Freeman and Medoff, *What Do Unions Do?*, 3, 4, 14).

"The union wage effect will typically lead to an inefficient allocation of society's labour, capital and other resources and thus to a reduction in the total income generated by the economy. This "deadweight loss" or allocative inefficiency comes about as follows. Starting, for conceptual purposes, in a situation in which wages and employment are determined by competitive market forces, raising wages in the union sector leads to a reduction in employment and output in that sector as firms substitute machinery and equipment and other inputs for union labour and consumers substitute away from the relatively more expensive union-produced goods and services. The supply of labour to the non-union sector will thus be increased, tending to lower wages and increase employment in that sector. Some individuals may drop out of the labour force as wages fall in the non-union sector and jobs are rationed in the union sector. The economy ends up with less labour (and more machinery and equipment) employed in the union sector and more labour (and less capital) employed in the non-union sector compared to the initial equilibrium.

The union/non-union wage differential results partly from the wages of union members being higher than they would be in a competitive market equilibrium and partly from the wages of non-union workers being lower than they would otherwise be. The misallocation of labour resources occurs because higher wages and reduced employment in the organized sector pushes other workers into less productive and more poorly paying jobs in the non-union sector" (Riddell, *Canadian Labour Relations*, 72).

15 The following examples illustrate the consensus about the favourable aspects of unions:
"A strong union, guided by farseeing men who have a grave sense of responsibility, is found to enable a few minutes' quite conversation to settle innumerable petty disputes that in old times would have caused much delay and worry and loss of mutual feeling ... In such trades we may conclude confidently that Trade Unions on the whole facilitate business" (Marshall, *Elements of Economics*, 381–2).

"The protection against the abuse of managerial authority given by seniority systems and grievance procedures seems to me to be a union accomplishment of the greatest importance. So too is the organized representation in public affairs given the worker by the political activities of unions" (Rees, *Economics of Trade Unions*, 186).

"Industrial relations experts have long stressed the ways in which collective bargaining can induce better management and higher productivity. These specialists note that unions can increase the development and retention of skills, provide information about what occurs on the shop floor, improve morale, and pressure management to be more efficient in its operations. Unionists point out that in addition to increasing wages, unions provide workers both with protection against arbitrary management decisions and with a voice at the work place and in the political arena ... the voice/response face of unionism suggests important ways in which unionism can raise productivity. First of all, voice at a workplace should reduce the rate of quitting. Since lower quit rates imply lower hiring and training costs and less disruption in the functioning of work groups, they should raise productivity. In addition, the likelihood that workers and firms will remain together for long periods of time should increase the incentive for investment in skills specific to an enterprise, which also raises productivity" (Freeman and Medoff, *What Do Unions Do?*, 3–4, 14).

"The positive consequences are associated primarily with the non-wage effects of collective bargaining and with providing a form of "industrial democracy" in the workplace" (Riddell, *Canadian Labour Relations*, 81).

16 Freeman and Medoff, *What Do Unions Do?*, chapter 16.
17 Riddell, *Canadian Labour Relations*, 81
18 Riddell, *Labour-Management Cooperation*, 3.
19 De Fina, "Unions, Relative Wages and Economic Efficiency."
20 Riddell, *Canadian Labour Relations*, 73
21 Freeman and Medoff, *What Do Unions Do?*, 57.
22 Riddell, *Work and Pay*, 18.
23 Ibid., 19.
24 Ibid., 23.
25 Capital stock means the total amount of physical capital, e.g. buildings and machinery, employed in production. Marginal product is the amount by which total output increases when one additional worker is employed. Average product is total output divided by the number of workers. It is normally a condition of equilibrium that marginal product be less than average product, for if one additional worker would add as much as the average product of existing workers, then if they are worth employing, he would be.

CHAPTER TWO

1 See, for example, Okun, *Equality and Efficiency.*
2 See, for example, Worland, *Scholasticism and Welfare Economics.*
3 The condition for profit maximization for the firm is that the marginal cost of labour equals the marginal revenue product of labour. If there is perfect competition in the product market, marginal revenue product equals the value of marginal product. If there is perfect competition in the labour market, the marginal cost of labour equals the wage rate. With both monopoly and monopsony, however, the value of marginal product is greater than marginal revenue product and the marginal cost of labour is greater than the wage rate. Thus with monopoly or monopsony, or both, the firm's maximum willingness to pay wages will be less than the customers' willingness to pay for the product.

4 See, for example, Okun, "Rational-Expectations-with-Misperceptions," 140:
"The costs of finding the most rewarding job are large for a worker;
the costs of obtaining the most productive worker are large for the
employer; and the benefits of experience on a particular job can
be substantial. These considerations promote continuing relationships with substantial bilateral monopoly surpluses. In some cases,
they lead to explicit contracts that fix the wage over a substantial
interval, even while not fixing the amount of employment. More
often, they lead to implicit contracts where the employer and the
worker conduct themselves and communicate with each other in
ways that help to make the continuation of the relationship worth-
while for both."

5 A survey of recent studies of the connection between unemployment insurance benefits and the level and duration of unemployment is in Riddell, *Work and Pay*. The 1971 revisions to the
Unemployment Insurance Act raised the NAIRU (nonaccelerating inflation rate of unemployment) by 1 to 2 percentage points (19).
The average duration of unemployment increased by one and a
half to two weeks (33). Subsequently benefits were made smaller
or more difficult to obtain, and these changes also had a significant effect on noncyclical unemployment (20).

6 Recent Canadian data on the provisions of collective agreements
concerning notice of termination, severance pay, and supplementary unemployment insurance benefits are contained in Gunderson,
"Alternative Mechanisms."

CHAPTER THREE

1 In practice the wage changes indicated by market theory may be
tempered by inertia, so that both wage changes and wage differentials may be less marked than the theory would suggest. Perceived
trends may result in wage adjustments during the life of a contract by a process of "wage drift." Expected inflation, for example,
may be the motive for wage adjustments that themselves contribute to the inflation. See, for example, Okun, "Invisible Handshake."

2 See, for example, ibid.

CHAPTER FOUR

1 Employers may refrain from exercising their power over committed
workers in order to avoid antagonizing them. See, for example,
Okun, "Rational-Expectations-with-Misperceptions," 140:

"Clearly, the firm that hires a worker with a career job in mind must lead him to believe that his position will gradually improve, and certainly not worsen. Once the firm paints a bright future in order to recruit that worker, any subsequent cut in wages must be a disappointment and a source of antagonism that would jeopardize the firm's investment in that worker. Hence the firm's inhibition about reducing wages has a sound, rational basis. In fact, when money wages normally rise over time, the same inhibitions can also apply to hold-downs or even slowdowns of wages for employees who have been recruited with the expectation of moving upward absolutely and keeping up relatively."

2 For a review of the literature on the boundaries of the bargaining range, and the process of bargaining within that range, see Chamberlain and Kuhn, *Collective Bargaining*, chapter 7.

3 The concept of countervailing power was developed in Galbraith, *American Capitalism*.

4 On the relative merits of short and long contracts see Riddell, *Canadian Labour Relations*, 43–4.

5 For a discussion of the relative efficiencies of the market mechanism and collective bargaining see Freeman and Medoff, *What Do Unions Do?*, chapter 6.

6 A static model relating the wage rate to the expected length of a strike by the "employer's concession curve" and the "union's resistance curve" was developed in Hicks, *Theory of Wages*, chapter 7. He argued that a dynamic process of bargaining may reach an outcome different from that indicated by the balance of static forces.

7 A discussion of the various techniques for influencing the cost of agreement and the cost of disagreement is contained in Chamberlain and Kuhn, *Collective Bargaining*, chapter 7.

8 For a discussion of the tactics of picketing and boycotts, see ibid., chapter 7.

9 The total cost of strikes and lock-outs is not easy to estimate because some of the cost is in the form of inconvenience to third parties that is impossible to measure. Most attempts at measurement are limited to direct working time lost by persons on strike. "In the decade from 1971 to 1980, just 2.6 percent of workers in the United States were on strike in a typical year, and just 0.18 percent of total working time was lost because of strikes – less time lost than that lost from worker absences for the common cold. Since most strikes occur in unionized sectors, however, the work loss under unionism is larger: in the 1980s about 11 percent of unionized workers went on strike in a typical year, reducing

work time by an average of 0.9 percent" (Freeman and Medoff, *What Do Unions Do?*, 217–18).

"Very little is known about the costs to society of strikes and lockouts. Compared to the fairly substantial (though as yet inconclusive) amount of research on the causes of strikes, the consequences have been largely ignored. The conventional wisdom among industrial relations scholars seems to be that the overall economic costs of work stoppage are small (see, e.g., Mitchell, 1981). There are several reasons for this belief. Total working time (and thus income and output) lost owing to strikes and lockouts is small in aggregate, both in absolute terms and relative to other causes of lost working time (absenteeism, workplace injuries and illnesses, and so on). Further, measured lost working time may overstate the total cost to society for several reasons. The firm may produce extra output and the workers earn extra income either before or after a work stoppage. In addition, other firms in the same or in a related industry may increase output and employment as consumers of the product or service switch to alternative sources. These factors reduce the net cost to society. At the same time, a strike or lockout can lead to a reduction in output and employment in other firms – usually suppliers or customers of the affected firm, or suppliers of the employees whose income is temporarily low. This reduced output and income due to a multiplier effect is not counted in the time lost measures" (Riddell, *Work and Pay*, 41).

10 The extent to which unions can succeed in raising wage rates has been controversial in the literature. Recent studies conclude that their effect is substantial. Canadian studies are reviewed in Riddell, *Canadian Labour Relations*, 70:
"The union wage effect is usually expressed in terms of the union/non-union wage differential, the wage difference between unionized and "comparable" non-union workers ... Although there is considerable variation in the magnitude of these estimates, reflecting different data sources, time period and methodologies, the empirical studies indicate that there is a significant difference between the wages of union and comparable non-union workers. For the economy as a whole, the union/non-union differential appears to be approximately 15–20 percent. It varies considerably across occupations, industries and other classifications of workers."

Kumar, "Union Growth in Canada," 105, reaches the following conclusion: "The available information suggests that unionized workers – that is, employees covered by collective agreements – receive higher wages, get more paid holidays and vacations, have better sick leave and other related paid absences, and are covered by improved private welfare and benefit plans; weekly hours of work, however, are similar for unionized and non-unionized employees." Comparable studies in the USA are reported in Freeman and Medoff, *What Do Unions Do?*, 20, 44, 46, 249. "On the wage side, unions have a substantial monopoly wage impact, but there is no single union/nonunion wage differential. The union wage effect is greater for less educated than more educated workers, for younger than for prime-age workers, and for junior than for senior workers, and it is greater in heavily organized industries and in regulated industries than in others. It increased in the 1970s as unionized workers won wage gains exceeding those of their non-union peers."; "In capsule form, the early work found a union wage effect of 10–15% on average, with considerable variation over time and among different groups of workers."; "while estimated union wage effects vary among surveys and groups covered, in all cases unionized labour is substantially more highly paid than non-unionized labor. In the 1970s, the archetypical union wage effect was on the order of 20 to 30 percent."; "Government policies aside, we believe that the burden of reducing the costs of the monopoly face of unionism, particularly the loss of jobs, lies with unionized labor and management. Unions pushed the union wage premium to extremely high levels from the mid-1970s to the early 1980s, gaining more and more for an increasingly small share of the workforce."

11 This effect in Europe is summarized as follows in Riddell, *Labour-Management Cooperation*, 39, 40:
"At present the European countries generally face a much more severe unemployment problem than North America. A growing number of economists and policy analysts believe that this unemployment is largely classical in nature – that is, results from real wages being above their equilibrium (full employment) levels. If this diagnosis is substantially correct, policies to reduce real wages will be effective in reducing unemployment while expansionary aggregate demand policies may be ineffective."
"According to this "Eurosclerosis" view, the substantial expansion of the welfare state in these countries, high minimum wages, restrictions on the ability of employers to dismiss redundant employees, and downward inflexibility of real wages due to explicit or implicit indexation severely inhibit the functioning and adaptability of labour and product markets, leading to reduced economic growth and high unemployment (Ellman, 1985). Thus, in addition to pressures to reduce real wages, there are also pressures to re-

duce the role of social insurance, indexation and the welfare state, and to increase flexibility in labour and product markets."

12 See, for example, Freeman and Medoff, *What Do Unions Do?*, 22: "Unionized employers tend to earn a lower rate of return per dollar of capital than do nonunion employers. The return is lower under unionism because the increase in wages and the greater amount of capital used per worker are not compensated for by the higher productivity of labor associated with unionism."

13 "If unions raise wage rates in a particular occupation or industry, they necessarily make the amount of employment available in the occupation or industry less than it otherwise would be – just as any higher price cuts down the amount purchased. The effect is an increased number of persons seeking other jobs, which forces down wages in other occupations. Since unions have generally been strongest among groups that would have been high-paid anyway, their effect has been to make high-paid workers higher paid at the expense of lower-paid workers. Unions have therefore not only harmed the public at large and workers as a whole by distorting the use of labor, they have also made the incomes of the working class more unequal by reducing the opportunities available to the most disadvantaged workers" (Friedman and Friedman, *Capitalism and Freedom*, 124, quoted in Freeman and Medoff, *What Do Unions Do?*, 16).

14 "This explains, at least in part, why unions emphasize seniority, which protects the older incumbent workers, and why they fight wage cuts even if that means layoffs. Such layoffs are likely to fall on the younger marginal workers, who are less likely to exert crucial political pressure and more likely to be mobile and have alternatives. When the possible layoffs threaten the jobs of the representative median voters, then concession bargaining and a willingness to engage in work sharing become more likely" (Gunderson, "Alternative Mechanism," 135).

15 "By favouring layoffs and employment reductions over alternative adjustment mechanisms – such as work sharing and wage reductions or other concessions – unions tend to increase the magnitude of the employment adjustments that result from a particular economic disturbance, thus shifting more of the cost of adjustment to public programs such as unemployment insurance, as well as to the individuals affected. This preference for employment reductions over alternative adjustment strategies is consistent with the view that unions represent primarily the preferences of older, more senior workers, whereas competitive market forces respond chiefly to the preferences of younger, more mobile workers. It is this

younger group that firms generally try to attract and retain. The fact that unions also raise wages above competitive market levels may also worsen adjustment problems, as workers laid off from well-paid jobs will remain unemployed longer in the hope that their former job returns" (Riddell, *Adapting to Change*, 11).

16 "Unionized workers not only receive better fringe benefits than comparable non-union workers, but unions raise the proportion of total compensation which is devoted to fringe benefits (Freeman, 1981). These benefits are generally worth more to more senior workers and to workers with a long expected tenure with the firm. Unionized firms rely more on temporary layoffs to respond to fluctuations in demand and these are generally by reverse seniority (Medoff, 1979). Promotions are based more on seniority in union firms and terminations are more likely to be on a last-in-first-out basis (Medoff and Abraham, 1981)" (Riddell, *Canadian Labour Relations*, 77).

17 "Those workers lucky enough to obtain employment in unionized firms will earn more, and comparable unorganized workers will earn less. Since unions tend to organize most successfully the larger firms in the economy, which tend to pay higher wages even in the absence of unions, this exacerbates income inequality. In addition, some of the most poorly paid occupations are not eligible for unionization and may have their living standards reduced further by higher prices for goods produced by union labour" (Riddell, *Canadian Labour Relations*, 73).

18 The extent of this problem is discussed in Riddell, *Work and Pay*, 24, 39:
"While a majority of youth find jobs relatively quickly after becoming unemployed, an important minority do not and this number accounts for much of the youth unemployment. Furthermore, a significant fraction of youth unemployment spells end in withdrawal from the labour force, so the total duration of joblessness is understated by our usual measure of labour force status.

Youth unemployment tends to be highest among the least educated, particularly school dropouts. For example, in 1982 the unemployment rate among youth aged 15 to 24 was 18.8 percent, but 32 percent among those with fewer than eight years of education and 10 percent among those with university education. Other factors accounting for prolonged periods of unemployment are location in areas of slow growth and high unemployment and lack of success at finding a first job."

"We can fully accept the equity objectives implicit in minimum wage legislation and yet feel the policy is unwise. Good intentions do not necessarily lead to good policies. The econometric evidence suggests that minimum wages are an ineffective and inefficient way of raising living standards among low wage earners. Thus, there are solid reasons to examine other approaches. In particular, two options – supplementing the income of the working poor and improving opportunities for training in order to raise productivity and earnings – seem preferable."

CHAPTER FIVE

1 A discussion of the power of organizations that are not responsible to the public to affect the public interest is contained in Chamberlain and Kuhn, *Collective Bargaining*, chapter 16.
2 For an excellent account of the forces leading to the development of the market system see Heilbroner, *Making of Economic Society*, especially chapter 4.
3 See, for example, McCallum, "Rational Expectations Theory."
4 See Friedman, "Role of Monetary Policy."
5 For a survey of the recent literature see Riddell, *Work and Pay*.
6 "To avoid misunderstanding, let me emphasize that by using the term "natural" rate of unemployment, I do not mean to suggest that it is immutable and unchangeable. On the contrary, many of the market characteristics that determine its level are man-made and policy-made. In the United States, for example, legal minimum wage rates, the Walsh-Healy and Davis-Bacon Acts, and the strength of labor unions all make the natural rate of unemployment higher than it would otherwise be. Improvements in employment exchanges, in availability of information about job vacancies and labor supply, and so on, would tend to lower the natural rate of unemployment. I use the term "natural" for the same reason Wicksell did – to try to separate the real forces from monetary forces" (Friedman, "Role of Monetary Policy," 9).
  The 'natural rate of unemployment' ... is not a numerical constant but depends on 'real' as opposed to monetary factors – the effectiveness of the labour market, the extent of competition or monopoly, the barriers or encouragements to working in various occupations, and so on" (Friedman, "Inflation and Unemployment").
7 The extent to which unions succeed in achieving higher wage rates than arise in nonunionized occupations has been controversial. For a discussion of the early debate in the economics literature see Hutt, *Theory of Collective Bargaining*.
  In the USA, data are now available separately for wage increases

in union agreements covering 1,000 or more workers and for average hourly earnings in all occupations (including both union and nonunion workers). Over the 1970–7 period union wage rates rose at an average rate of 8.2 per cent while the index of average hourly earnings rose by 7.3 per cent. Wage and salary increases in occupations covered by collective bargaining agreements in 1976 and 1977 were 8.1 per cent and 7.6 per cent. Increases in occupations not covered were 6.8 per cent and 6.6 per cent in the same years. See, Perry, "Slowing the Wage-Price Spiral," in Okun and Perry, *Curing Chronic Inflation.* In the introduction to that volume the editors state:
"On the whole, union members obtained real wage increases during the 1970s that matched their average rate of gain during the previous decade, whereas this was not true for non-union workers as a group." Riddell, *Canadian Labour Relations,* 11, comments on the Canadian experience as follows: " Because non-union wages appear to be more flexible downward than union wages, employment growth in the union sector may well be slower than in the economy as a whole. The union/non-union wage differential tends to be largest in periods of slow growth at the expense of union firms. This phenomenon has been seen most vividly in the depressed construction industry in western Canada in recent years."

8 The effect of unions on profits is discussed in Freeman and Medoff, *What Do Unions Do?,* 189, 247–8: "What unions do to profits can be easily summarized: in general, they reduce profitability, especially in the more monopolized sectors of US industry"; "While our research suggests that unionism generally serves as a force for social and economic good, it has also found that unions benefit labor at the expense of capital. Unions reduce the profitability of organized firms, particularly those in concentrated sectors where profits are abnormally high."

9 The following example, from which readers can draw their own conclusions, was reported in the *Globe and Mail,* 4 October 1986, 12:
"People fought the odds to the very end last night to land a job at a new auto plant. During the unusual week-long recruitment drive to fill 3,000 positions with American Motors (Canada) Ltd. in nearby Brampton, company officials said they distributed nearly 60,000 applications. The drive-through application centre was set upon Monday in the parking lot of the otherwise deserted grounds of Canada's Wonderland near this community north of Toronto. Despite a week of mainly rainy weather, people from across the country lined up to get applications for the jobs that will pay

$13 and hour and up when the plant opens in December. American Motors and Canada Employment will process the application forms and invite a "selected few" for interviews. This will be followed by an aptitude test and on-the-job training at the plant when it opens."

10 The extent to which the unemployment problem is attributable to wage rates that are too high is difficult to assess and impossible to measure precisely. The official unemployment rate ranges in the order of 10 per cent of the labour force, but this includes persons transitionally unemployed in the process of changing jobs. Since some period of search activity is efficient, the optimal rate of unemployment is not 0, though it is much less than 10 per cent. In addition to those officially unemployed are those who have withdrawn from the labour force in frustration because they have given up hope of finding work in the current labour market, or who are underemployed in jobs that do not make efficient use of their skills. The numbers whose prospects of efficient employment are diminished by the effects of high real wages are impossible to measure, but are certainly significant.

CHAPTER SIX

1 Specialized high salary workers fare worse in the public sector than the private, while less specialized low wage workers are better paid in the public sector. See, for example, Riddell, *Canadian Labour Relations:* "Comparison of wage levels indicates that, in recent years, public sector employees have typically enjoyed a compensation advantage over "comparable" workers in the private sector ... The size of this compensation advantage varies considerably across groups of employees: it is largest for females and low wage workers, and smallest – often, indeed, a disadvantage – for employees at higher salary levels."

2 The extent to which unionization of public sector workers is permitted varies among jurisdictions, as does the use of collective bargaining and the right to strike. The growth of public sector unions in Canada since the 1960s, the effect of that growth on wage rates, and the differences from the public sectors in the USA and the UK are discussed in Riddell, *Canadian Labour Relations.*

3 "A fundamental problem remains in public sector wage policy – that of separating the government's role as employer from that as protector of the public interest. The recent public sector wage restraint programs illustrate this difficulty. From the public interest perspective, this approach can be argued to have had some justifi-

cation as a limited form of incomes policy designed to help reduce inflation, though whether it was effective is another matter. However, governments generally did not distinguish this purpose from that of controlling the costs of providing public services in a period of reduced revenues" (Riddell, *Canadian Labour Relations*, 28).

4 "A review of the existing literature and empirical evidence on public sector wage settlements leads one to draw the following three conclusions concerning public sector wage compensation. First, over the 1967–83 time period, wage settlements in the public sector have not exceeded wage settlements in the private sector. In fact, average wage increases obtained by public sector workers have been four-tenths of one percent lower each year than wage increases obtained by private sector employees (based on Labour Canada's collective bargaining research files). Second, the economic structure of wage settlements in the public sector (excluding arbitrated settlements) is not dissimilar to the structure of wage settlement in the private sector. In particular, there is no clear empirical evidence that public sector wage rate increases have been less responsive to labour market conditions than wage changes in the private sector. In fact, average wage settlements in the public and private sectors have moved in a very similar cyclical manner over the 1968–83 period. Finally, there is no empirical evidence that public sector wage settlements will, in general, spill over into the private sector and permeate throughout the entire economy" (Wilton, "Public Sector Wage Compensation," 281).

5 On the basis of 1971 census data, Gunderson found that: "[T]he pure surplus or economic rent that public sector workers received relative to their private sector counterparts was $492, or 6.2%, for males and $383, or 8.6% for females. The public sector wage advantage was larger for low-wage workers, illustrating the basic dilemma that policies to curb the advantage may conflict with the desire to raise the wages of low-wage workers and achieve equal pay for equal work between males and females" (Gunderson, "Earnings Differentials," 228).

6 "[T]he overall public/private sector wage differential can primarily, perhaps entirely, be accounted for by the higher union density in the public sector" (Riddell, *Canadian Labour Relations*, 27).

CHAPTER SEVEN

1 "[T]he strike threat system is an anomaly. It is analogous to the medieval method of dispute resolution known as trial by combat. When two parties had a dispute, they would physically confront

171 Notes to pages 127–133

each other. The winner of the test of strength was declared to be in the right by virtue of his victory. The assumption was that a higher power had provided the victor with the wherewithal to prevail and by doing so had indicated the virtuous one. Under democracy, disputes should be settled by reference to appropriated standards, not by the imposition of raw power or by the mysterious intervention of God. However, under the strike-threat system, winners and losers are determined by factors such as technology, business cycles and strike funds, not by reference to relevant objective standards. Moreover, the ability to pose (or withstand) a strike threat is not equitably distributed. Some parties have a lot of clout (autoworkers, for example) while others have very little (clerks in small retail stores, for example), but the distribution has nothing to do with democratic values. In short, the strike threat system is a very inadequate device for ensuring that all employee-citizens have the capacity to participate in decisions which critically affect their working lives" (Adams, "Two Policy Approaches to Labour-Management Decision Making," 103).

2 "[I]t is probably accurate to state that the essential difference between negotiating under the strike or lockout threat and under the arbitration threat is that with the former the parties estimate the concession behaviour of each other based on the cost of a work stoppage to each, while with the latter they estimate what an arbitrator is likely to view a fair settlement" (Riddell, *Canadian Labour Relations*, 50–1).

3 "Although its use varies across jurisdictions, arbitration is widely used among hospital workers, police, firefighters, teachers, and government employees. In some instances arbitration is imposed by statute; in others, the parties may choose it and occasionally it is imposed on an ad hoc basis as part of back-to-work legislation in particular disputes. Its two main forms are conventional arbitration, in which the arbitrator chooses an award after hearing arguments and evidence from the two parties, and final-offer arbitration, in which the arbitrator, after receiving briefs and hearing evidence, must choose either the employer's or the union's final offer. Conventional arbitration is by far the most widely employed system in Canada. In the United States there has been more experimentation with final-offer arbitration and its variants" (Riddell, *Canadian Labour Relations*, 49).

4 "Under arbitration, whether conventional or final-offer, the negotiating parties will focus on what the arbitrator is likely to view as an appropriate award. If there is little "arbitral uncertainty," the arbitrator's notion of an appropriate award becomes the "threat

point" in bargaining; neither will agree to an outcome any worse than this award. Thus, if they settle, the outcome negotiated under either the threat of conventional or final-offer arbitration will be dictated by the arbitrator's view of the appropriate award. With uncertainly about the arbitrator's views, risk averse parties become more likely to settle. Even in this case, however, there is reason to believe that the negotiating parties will be substantially influenced by what they think the arbitrator thinks is appropriate" (Riddell, *Canadian Labour Relations*, 50).

5 Arbitration of industrial disputes has been the standard practice in New Zealand since 1894 and in Australia since 1904. There have, of course, been many controversial issues and several amendments to the structure, procedure, and criteria. That such systems have survived throughout the twentieth century demonstrates their viability. While there are always pressures for change, there has been no serious argument for the abolition of the principle of arbitration. Public opinion in Australia has been summarized as follows: "So far as can be seen, at almost any time, there is a strong feeling against the system in operation, coupled with a fairly consistent faith in compulsory arbitration as a method" (International Labour Office, "Conciliation and Arbitration in Industrial Disputes," Studies and Reports Series A, no. 34 (Geneva, 1933), quoted by Walker in Loewenberg et al., *Compulsory Arbitration*, 35). Careful study of the experience of New Zealand and Australia would yield valuable guidance in the framing of comparable Canadian legislation. Among the descriptions, studies, and assessments of those systems are the following: Woods, *Industrial Conciliation and Arbitration*; Healey, *Federal Arbitration in Australia*; Foenander, *Industrial Conciliation and Arbitration*; Timbs, *Towards Wage Justice*. The Australian system is also discussed in Loewenberg et al., *Compulsory Arbitration*.

6 Concern has been expressed in the literature that the availability of arbitration may deter serious negotiation and reduce the likelihood of agreement between the parties. Bargaining may be impeded by both the "chilling effect" and the "narcotic effect." See Gunderson, *Economic Aspects of Interest Arbitration*. The evidence is summarized by Riddell, *Canadian Labour Relations*, 49:
"Arbitration, like the strike or lockout, is intended to be used infrequently, in those circumstances where the two parties were unable to reach agreement. An important consideration, then, is the effect of arbitration on the incentives of each side to make concessions and, ultimately, to converge on a settlement. One concern is that the existence of arbitration as a dispute resolution

mechanism would reduce the incentives to reach a negotiated settlement, a possibility referred to as the "chilling effect" of arbitration. This would occur, for example, if arbitrators tended to "split the difference" between the two parties' positions. More generally, the parties may be reluctant to make concessions if some weight is given to their final offers by the arbitrator. Another concern is that with arbitration as the ultimate mechanism for choosing a settlement, one or both parties will simply "go through the motions" and withhold the time and effort required for serious negotiations. Over time, both might rely more and more on arbitration to determine wages and working conditions, a possibility referred to as the "narcotic effect" of arbitration.

Evidence for the validity of these concerns is inconclusive. There is some which suggests that the narcotic and chilling effects may operate. However, there is also conflicting evidence, and there is not complete agreement on the appropriate methodology for testing for these effects. If these effects do occur, however, they occur so slowly and mildly that debate continues on their existence. Thus, there is little evidence to support the view that collective bargaining will disappear when arbitration is available as the dispute resolution mechanism."

In Australia, where compulsory arbitration is available in all disputes, most are in fact resolved by agreement. See Loewenberg et al., *Compulsory Arbitration*, 21. The greater the proportion of the costs of arbitration that would be borne by the parties, the greater would be the incentive for them to reach agreement without recourse to arbitration.

7 "It is true that with unionization come higher compensation levels than would otherwise exist, and this development somewhat elevates the costs of providing schools, hospitals and other public services. This is one of the effects of collective bargaining, and it exists in the private sector as well as in the public sector. Just as extensive unionization in the automobile industry raises the price of cars to consumers, so unionization among government employees raises the cost of public services. There does not appear to be any reason to treat one group differently from another on these grounds alone" (Riddell, *Canadian Labour Relations*, 28).

CHAPTER EIGHT

1 In Canada, jurisdiction over labour relations is divided between the federal and provincial levels of government. The recommendations made here are applicable to both levels. Ideally, comparable legis-

lation would be adopted at the federal level and by all ten provinces. In practice, it is unlikely that eleven governments would act simultaneously. There is however, no reason why these recommendations should not be adopted by the federal government for all matters concerning employment contracts under its jurisdiction before any provincial government passes similar legislation. Nor is there any reason why a single province should not proceed before the federal government or other provinces. Whichever government acts first, the resulting experience will guide other governments that may subsequently adopt similar legislation. Experiments that succeed are likely to be emulated. Canada has a long history of being governed by multiple governments and there exists considerable diversity in current legislation. The differences that would exist with an arbitration service in some jurisdictions but not in others would create no great problem. Much would be learned from comparative studies of different systems that would serve as valuable guidance for all. The proposals made here are relevant to all eleven jurisdictions whether they act separately or together.

2 In addition to our own experience, we can benefit from that of other countries, especially New Zealand and Australia. See note 5, chapter 6.

3 One major criticism of the Australian system is that no criteria are stipulated by statute beyond vague references to equity, goodwill, and the public interest. See Loewenberg et al., *Compulsory Arbitration*, 22, 29.

4 There is currently much debate concerning the principle of "equal pay for work of equal value." It is not clear exactly what the advocates of this principle mean by "work of equal value," but it is clear that the objective sought is equity rather than efficiency. Efficiency requires that the price charged an employer for the use of labour should equal its opportunity cost. This principle could be described as "equal pay for labour of equal alternative value to the society." As a principle of efficiency it is firmly based in the economic concept of opportunity cost. It should not be confused with the vague concepts of equity inherent in the arguments for "equal pay for work of equal value." If "equal value" means equal value of marginal product, then both principles would be satisfied in a perfectly competitive labour market, but it is not clear that this is the meaning currently associated with "equal value." Wage rates that satisfied any other meaning of "equal value" would violate the basic condition of efficiency.

5 The proposal that arbitrated wage rates should reflect the existence of surpluses and shortages of labour in the labour market is not new. Early in this century arbitrated wages in the UK were

based on "the final overriding principle that the pay should be such as to attract and retain a sufficient number of entrants" (Ford, *Economics of Collective Bargaining*, 97). Subsequently principles of equity, comparability, and ability to pay came to dominate the principle of need to pay. Recent studies of arbitration in the USA and Canada have found the main criteria used to be comparability with wages earned by similar workers, changes in the cost of living, and the employer's ability to pay (Riddell, *Canadian Labour Relations*, 51). Gunderson has advocated the use of a market criterion in public sector wage arbitration:
"[W]age rates that are too high, relative to their private-sector counterparts or for the requirements of the jobs, result in excess supplies of workers for those jobs. Conversely, wage rate that are too low result in shortages of workers" (Gunderson, *Interest Arbitration*, 43).
Riddell supports his proposal:
"One criterion for guiding arbitrators that merits more consideration is the use of measures of labour market disequilibrium (Gunderson, 1983). The relative magnitude of queues and shortages can provide valuable information on the extent to which relative wages are too high or too low. Incorporating this type of information is a practical option for injecting more market rationale into the arbitration process" (Riddell, *Canadian Labour Relations*, 51).

6 The consistent application of criteria prescribed by statute should overcome the inconsistencies that characterize our *ad hoc* use of arbitration. Recent studies have found that " there is considerable variability across arbitrators in the awards chosen in identical circumstances" (Riddell, *Canadian Labour Relations*, 50).

7 "Predictions that collective bargaining would wither away with the use of arbitration have not been realized. Wage settlements negotiated under arbitration or under the threat of arbitration are likely to depend more on factors such as compensation comparability and the cost of living, and less on the relative bargaining power of the two sides ... Fears that collective bargaining would wither away when arbitration was the dispute resolution mechanism seem to have been exaggerated" (Riddell, *Canadian Labour Relations*, 51, 53).

8 "[S]ome Canadian jurisdictions (notably British Columbia, Quebec, Manitoba, and some federal industries) have recently required first-contract arbitration when a new union has been certified but the parties cannot agree to a first contract" (Gunderson, *Interest Arbitration*, 60). "Why not a system where second, third or fourth contracts could be arbitrated?" (Adams, "Two Policy Approaches to Labour-Management Decision Making," 103).

Bibliography

Adams, R.J. "Two Policy Approaches to Labour-Management
Decision Making at the Level of the Enterprise." In *Labour-
Management Cooperation in Canada*. Research coordinator W.C.
Riddell. Research studies prepared for the Royal Commission on
the Economic Union and Development Prospects for Canada, vol.
15. Toronto: University of Toronto Press 1985.

Baily, M.N., and A.M. Okun, eds. *The Battle Against
Unemployment and Inflation*. New York: Norton 1982.

Chamberlain, N.W., and J.W. Kuhn. *Collective Bargaining*. 2d ed.
New York: McGraw-Hill 1965.

De Fina, R.H., "Unions, Relative Wages and Economic Efficiency."
Journal of Labour Economics (October 1983) 408–29.

Ellman, M., "Eurosclerosis?" In *Unemployment, Can It Be
Reduced? An International Perspective*. Edited by N. Meltz and
S. Ostry. Toronto: University of Toronto Press. Forthcoming.

Foenander, O. De R., *Industrial Conciliation and Arbitration in
Australia*. Sydney: The Law Book Co. of Australia 1959.

Ford, P., *The Economics of Collective Bargaining*. Oxford: Basil
Blackwell 1964.

Freeman, R.B., "The Effects of Trade Unions on Fringe Benefits."
Industrial and Labour Relations Review (July 1981): 489–509.

Freeman, R.B. and J.L. Medoff. *What Do Unions Do?* New York:
Basic Books 1984.

Friedman, M. "The Role of Monetary Policy." *American Economic
Review* 58, no. 1 (March 1968): 1–17.

– "Inflation and Unemployment." The Nobel Foundation, 1976.
Reprinted in *The Battle Against Unemployment and Inflation*.
Edited by M.N. Baily and A.M. Okun. New York: Norton
1982.

Friedman, M., and R. Friedman. *Capitalism and Freedom.* Chicago: University of Chicago Press 1962.

Galbraith, J.K. *American Capitalism: The Concept of Countervailing Power.* Boston: Houghton Mifflin, 1952.

Gunderson, M. "Earnings Differentials Between the Public and Private Sectors." *Canadian Journal of Economics* (1979): 228–42.

– *Economic Aspects of Interest Arbitration.* Toronto: Ontario Economic Council 1983.

– "Alternative Mechanisms for Dealing with Permanent Layoffs, Dismissals, and Plant Closings." In *Adapting to Change: Labour Market Adjustment in Canada.* Research coordinator W.C. Riddell. Research Studies prepared for the Royal Commission on the Economic Union and Development Prospects for Canada, vol. 18. Toronto, University of Toronto Press 1985.

Hayek, F.A. *A Tiger by the Tail.* London: Institute of Economic Affairs 1972.

Healey, B. *Federal Arbitration in Australia.* Australia: Georgian House 1972.

Heilbroner, R.L. *The Making of Economic Society.* Englewood Cliffs, NJ: Prentice-Hall, 1962.

Hicks, J.R. *The Theory of Wages.* London: Macmillan 1932.

Hutt, W.H. *The Theory of Collective Bargaining.* Glencoe, Illinois: The Free Press 1954.

Krahn, H. and G. Lowe. "Public Attitudes Towards Unions: Some Canadian Evidence." *Journal of Labour Research,* 5, no. 2 (1984): 149–64.

Kumar, P. "Union Growth in Canada: Retrospect and Prospect." In *Canadian Labour Relations.* Research coordinator W.C. Riddell. Research studies prepared for the Royal Commission on the Economic Union and Development Prospects for Canada, vol. 16. Toronto: University of Toronto Press 1985.

Loewenberg, J.J. and W.J. Gershenfeld, H.J. Glasbeek, B.A. Hepple, and K.F. Walker. *Compulsory Arbitration: An International Comparison.* Lexington, Mass.: D.C. Heath 1976.

Marshall, A.T. *Elements of Economics.* London: Macmillan 1899.

McCallum, B.T. "The significance of Rational Expectations Theory." *Challenge.* January/February 1980. Reprinted as "Rational Expectations." In *The Battle Against Unemployment and Inflation.* Edited by M.N. Baily and A.M. Okun. New York: Norton 1982.

Medoff, J.L. "Layoffs and Alternatives Under Trade Unions in US Manufacturing." *American Economic Review* (June 1969): 380–95.

Medoff, J.L. and K.G. Abraham. "Involuntary Termination under Explicit and Implicit Employment Contracts." Cambridge, Mass.: Harvard University Press 1981. Mimeo.

Meltz, N. and S. Ostry, eds. *Unemployment: Can It Be Reduced? An International Perspective.* Toronto: University of Toronto Press. Forthcoming.

Mitchell, D.J.B. "Collective Bargaining and the Economy." In US *Industrial Relations 1950–1980: A Critical Assessment.* Edited by J. Steiber et al. Madison, Wisconsin: Industrial Relations Research Association 1981.

Okun, A.M. *Equality and Efficiency, The Big Tradeoff.* Washington, DC: Brookings 1975.

– "Rational-Expectations-with-Misperceptions as the Theory of the Business Cycle." In *Economics for Policy Making, Selected Essays of Arthur M. Okun.* Edited by J.A. Pechman. Cambridge, Mass.: MIT Press 1983.

– "The Invisible Handshake and the Inflationary Process." In *Economics for Policy Making, Selected Essays of Arthur M. Okun.* Edited by J.A. Pechman. Cambridge, Mass.: MIT Press 1983.

Okun, A.M. and G.L. Perry. *Curing Chronic Inflation.* Washington, DC: Brookings 1978.

Pechman, J.A. ed. *Economics for Policy Making, Selected Essays of Arthur M. Okun.* Cambridge, Mass.: MIT Press 1983.

Perry, G.L. "Slowing the Wage-Price Spiral: The Macroeconomic View." In *Curing Chronic Inflation.* Edited by A.M. Okun and G.L. Perry. Washington, DC: Brookings 1978.

Rees, A. *The Economics of Trade Unions.* Rev. ed. Chicago: University of Chicago Press 1977.

Riddell, W.C., research coordinator. *Labour-Management Cooperation in Canada.* Research Studies prepared for the Royal Commission on the Economic Union and Development Prospects for Canada, vol 15. Toronto: University of Toronto Press 1985.

– *Canadian Labour Relations.* Research studies prepared for the Royal Commission on the Economic Union and Development Prospects for Canada, vol. 16. Toronto: University of Toronto Press 1985.

– *Work and Pay: The Canadian Labour Market.* Research studies prepared for the Royal Commission on the Economic Union and Development Prospects for Canada, vol. 17. Toronto: University of Toronto Press 1985.

– *Adapting to Change: Labour Market Adjustment in Canada.* Research studies prepared for the Royal Commission on the

Economic Union and Development Prospects for Canada, vol. 18. Toronto: University of Toronto Press 1985.

Timbs, J.N. *Towards Wage Justice by Judicial Regulation: An Appreciation of Australia's Experience under Compulsory Arbitration.* Louvain: Institut de recherche économique, sociales et politiques 1963.

Wilton, D.A. "Public Sector Wage Compensation. In *Canadian Labour Relations.* Research coordinator W.C. Riddell. Research studies prepared for the Royal Commission on the Economic Union and Development Prospects for Canada, vol. 16. Toronto, University of Toronto Press 1985.

Woods, N.S. *Industrial Conciliation and Arbitration in New Zealand.* Wellington: R.E. Owen, Government Printer 1963.

Worland, S.T. *Scholasticism and Welfare Economics.* Notre Dame, Indiana: University of Notre Dame Press 1967.

Index

aggregate demand, 91
allocation of labour.
See labour
anticombines legislation, 125
arbitration, 28, 126–37;
binding, 134, 136;
chilling and narcotic
effects, 172n6; compulsory, 67, 79, 87,
95, 132; conventional, 171n3; costs of,
134; criteria for, 128,
140, 142–7, 150,
175n5; final offer,
171n3; predictability
of, 171n4; in public
sector, 171n3; right
to, 148–51; voluntary,
131–2, 142
arbitration service,
139–42
arbitrators, 139
arms, right to bear, 128
Australia, 172n5,
173n6, 174n3
average product, 8–9,
160n25

balance of power, 62,
95, 117, 128
bankruptcy, 74
bargaining: costs, 57,
67; power, 78, 95;

range, 73, 76,
115–16, 162n2
barrier to entry, 58
bilateral monopoly, 86,
161n4
binding arbitration,
134, 136
boycott, 67, 162n8

capital, 72–3, 80, 110;
human, 11–13, 27–8;
return to, 165n12;
stock of, 9, 160n25
captive labour force,
58–9. *See also*
monopsony
case law, 133, 140. *See*
also precedent
casual labour, 30. *See*
also spot market
chilling effect, 175n7
classical economics, 8,
91
closure of firm, 74
coercion, 123, 128, 139
COLA, 51. *See also*
indexation
collective bargaining,
53–83, 122–5; constraint on, 119; defence of, 97; efficiency of, 67–77; equity
of, 77–80; extent of,
3; influence of, 3;

integrity, 80–3; in
public sector, 107–8,
114; reason for, 52
collusion, 60
comparative statics,
62–3
competitive market,
37, 48, 53–5, 62,
86, 6. *See also*
perfect competition
compulsory arbitration.
See arbitration
conciliation, 87, 127,
133, 149
conflict, 123; cost of,
5, 64–5, 68, 128;
dynamics of, 62,
162n6; public
interest in, 95, 124
contract, 119, 129. *See*
also law of contract
contract period, 31–2
controls. *See* wage
controls
conventional arbitration, 171n3
convergence of offers,
65–6, 68
countervailing power,
62, 106, 126, 162n3
criminal law, 120
criteria. *See* arbitration,
efficiency, equity,
integrity